Garuda Indon
The Building of a Nation

JOZEF MOLS

KEY
Books

AIRLINES SERIES, VOLUME 1

Title page image: A Boeing 777-300ER in flight. (Björn Van Brussel)

Contents page image: Garuda Airbus A330-300 arriving at Denpasar Airport. (Jozef Mols)

Published by Key Books
An imprint of Key Publishing Ltd
PO Box 100
Stamford
Lincs PE19 1XQ

www.keypublishing.com

The right of Jozef Mols to be identified as the author of this book has been asserted in accordance with the Copyright, Designs and Patents Act 1988 Sections 77 and 78.

Copyright © Jozef Mols, 2021

ISBN 978 1 913870 58 4

Typeset by SJmagic DESIGN SERVICES, India.

Contents

Introduction and Acknowledgements

Garuda Indonesia Airways is a fascinating airline, not only because it was set up at the end of World War Two and the War of Independence that followed, but also because it helped the emerging Republic of Indonesia to unify the many different populations on the more than 17,000 islands in the archipelago. As such, we can say the airline was an essential tool in the building of the nation. Later on, Garuda, of course, encountered many problems, like most state-owned airlines did. Government interference tied the hands of the management. Subsequently, both internal and external factors caused problems and crises. But each time, Garuda managed to counter the tide and stand up again. Therefore, this airline deserves a better look, and I hope this book will contribute to a better understanding of the airline's evolution.

But, how does one tell the story of a company that is older than oneself; an airline that is more than 70 years' old and whose origins go back to World War Two and the Civil War that followed? Many documents that could shed light on these early days were lost or destroyed. Only a few witnesses remain, but their memories have faded away, and whatever remains may be seasoned by the spices of imagination, personal perception or even self-interest or political and economical reasons. But this makes the story even more interesting for the storyteller and the reader.

When I had the pleasure of living in Indonesia for several years, the importance of air transportation in this enormous archipelago was clear. Without air transportation, it would never have been possible to create a country like Indonesia in the first place. Connectivity is one of the means that unites people living on more than 17,000 different islands, speaking more than 400 different languages and belonging to many ethnic and religious groups. An airline was one of the ingredients in the process of building a nation. And an aeroplane gave me the opportunity to discover the enormous and fascinating world that is Indonesia today.

Writing this book would not have been possible without the help of many people and organisations, both in Indonesia and abroad. I am very grateful to all of them for their assistance. First of all, I would like to thank the few survivors of the 'early days' of the airline for their information and eye-witness accounts. I also thank the Directorate General of Civil Aviation (Direktorat Jenderal Perhubungan Udara) for giving me unrestricted access to all of the civil aviation airports in Indonesia, both airside and landside. During these visits, I was not only able to take many of the pictures used in this book, but also to talk to Garuda's staff and technicians, which added to my knowledge about the airline. For the same reason, I thank the (then) station manager of KLM in Jakarta for making available an office at the Jakarta Soekarno-Hatta International Airport to conduct interviews. And, of course, I want to thank everybody – both private individuals and institutions – that allowed me to use their photographs to illustrate this book.

Jozef Mols

Chapter 1

The Building of a Nation

Many airlines that have been established since the 1960s and 1970s came into existence because private investors thought it would be possible for them to make profits by filling gaps in the existing transportation market. The 1960s was also the period during which workers could start enjoying paid holidays, thus increasing the demand for international (air) travel. This booming demand for holidays in sunny and exotic spots around the globe created the need to establish new airlines and to expand the services of existing ones.

In Third World countries, however, and certainly in those that gained independence recently – and mostly in the aftermath of World War Two – the establishment of airlines was mostly dictated by national interest, rather than by demand from the leisure market. Garuda Indonesia is a good example of such an airline, created by the need to establish domestic airline transportation and, by doing so, contribute to the 'building of a nation'. The development of an efficient air transportation industry in Indonesia was crucial because of the country's unique geographic situation. Indonesia is the world's largest archipelago, stretching for more than 3,100 miles between the westernmost point of Sumatra and the easternmost point in Irian Jaya. Of its more than 16,000 islands, nearly 6,000 are inhabited by more than 270 million people of different ethnic backgrounds, speaking about 400 different languages and dialects and who profess a whole series of religions.

The archipelago's strategic sea-lane position fostered inter-island and international trade, including commerce with Indian kingdoms and Chinese dynasties. Trade has since fundamentally shaped Indonesian history. Because of the geographic position of the archipelago and its renown for agriculture and trade, Portuguese traders, led by Francisco Serrao, sought to monopolise the sources of nutmeg, cloves and pepper in the Maluki Islands of the archipelago. They were followed by Dutch and British traders. In 1602, the Netherlands established the Verenigde Oost-Indische Companie (VOC) (Dutch East India Company) and became the dominant European power for almost 200 years. When in 1800, the VOC declared bankruptcy, the Netherlands established the Dutch East Indies as a nationalised colony. For most of the colonial period, Dutch control was tenuous, and Dutch forces were engaged in quelling rebellions. The influence of local leaders such as Prince Diponegoro in central Java, Imam Bonjol in central Sumatra and Pattimura in Maluku tied up the colonial forces. And in the early 20th century, Dutch dominance extended to what was to become Indonesia's current borderline. Nevertheless, the cry for independence could still be heard on most of the islands, but especially in Java and Sumatra. Independence movements, however, were suppressed, often ending in bloodshed.

KLM was one of the first airlines in the world to start up flights to the Dutch colonies. Established in 1919, KLM sent former general Cornelis Jacobus Snijders to the East Indies in 1920 in order to investigate the possibility of starting up flights within the archipelago. The Dutch government, however, which was supposed to finance this operation, was not interested. Frustrated by this decision, a group of Dutch entrepreneurs with interests in the colonies set up the Nederlands-Indische Luchtvaart Onderneming (NILO) (Dutch-East-Indian Aviation Company). The first flight of the new airline resulted in disaster. With a German-built LVG-C-VI, the NILO intended to fly from Batavia (Jakarta) to Surabaya via Semarang. Immediately after take-off, however, the aircraft crashed, killing three out of the four occupants. The cause of the accident became clear very soon: the aircraft was a two-seater, but NILO had four people on board this flight. The first flight of NILO also became its last one.

In the meantime, the Dutch–Indian government voted in a law stating that domestic airline transportation would only be allowed for airlines with their head offices in the colonies. If KLM wanted to start up such flights, it would first have to set up a subsidiary with a seat in East India. In 1925, a request for a concession by KLM was not accepted by the authorities in Batavia. The local government indeed refused to build airports for KLM and also refused to pay an annual subsidy of 613,000 guilders. Instead, private investors decided to set up a new domestic airline with a seat in Bandung and with a share capital of 5 million guilders. Shareholders were the mining company Billiton, the family Van Heek (textiles), the KPM shipping consortium, the Stork machine factory, the NHM (Nederlandse Handelsmaatschappij) and the Deli Company. Originally, the airline was to be named the NILM (Nederlands-Indische Luchtvaartmaatschappij), but later the name was changed to KNILM (with the 'K' for 'Koninklijk' or 'Royal') in order to avoid confusion with another existing company: the Nillmij insurance company. The new airline immediately bought four Fokker F.VIIIa/3m aircraft. Its agreement with the local government stipulated the airline would have to operate a daily Batavia–Semarang–Surabaya service and, from 1929, a weekly Batavia–Singapore flight via Belawan near Medan. The reason for the choice of Belawan might sound strange, but there was good reason: in Medan, the local horse racetrack was used as an airfield, and this would mean that each time a race would be held, the aircraft would not be able to land. So, another field in Belawan was selected.

Gradually, the services were expanded to include other islands in the archipelago, including Palembang and Medan in Sumatra, Balikpapan and Tarakan in Kalimantan and Denpasar in Bali. Immediately before the outbreak of the Pacific War, the KNILM also created a network in the eastern part of the East Indies archipelago, linking Batavia with destinations like Ambon. For this purpose, amphibious aircraft were used because of the lack of airstrip facilities in the region. In 1930, the KNILM started international operations with a flight to Singapore, followed in 1938 by operations to Sydney, stopping in Darwin, Cloncurry and Charleville. However, KNILM did not fly to the Netherlands, as this route was served by KLM.

During the Japanese attacks on the Dutch East Indies, KNILM was utilised for evacuation flights and transport of troops. On 28 December 1941, a KNILM Douglas DC-3 (PK-ALN) was destroyed on the ground by Japanese fighters at Medan, killing all crew members and passengers. All KNILM aircraft with sufficient range were evacuated to Australia. On 7 March 1942, one day before the capitulation of the island of Java, the last KNILM aircraft took off from Bandung. A number of KNILM aircraft were destroyed by the Japanese during bombing raids on Darwin. In all, 11 KNILM aircraft managed to escape to Australia including three Douglas DC-5s, two Douglas DC-3s, two Douglas DC-2s and three Model 14 Super Electras. In mid-May 1942, the remaining aircraft were sold to the American military. By the end of the war, some aircraft were integrated in the 18th Transport Squadron in Balikpapan and the 19th Transport Squadron in Brisbane.

If one looks at the KNILM statistics, one has to conclude that the importance of the airline is largely overestimated. Indeed, only colonial administrators dared to travel on the airline, mainly for business purposes but also for leisure. For the local population, flying with KNILM was not safe. They indeed made their own explanation for the name of the airline: 'Kalo Naik Ini Lekas Mati' or 'who enters a KNILM plane will soon die'. Therefore, one can conclude that KNILM's contribution to the work of the Dutch colonial powers was mainly important in the fields of cargo-transportation and transportation of mail.

The horse racetrack in Medan was used as an airstrip to welcome Dutch aircraft, flying to Indonesia. This photo was taken in 1924. (Nationaal Archief)

Arrival of the first flight by a Fokker F.VII at Medan Airport on 24 November 1924. (Tropenmuseum)

Arrival of the Fokker F.XVIII *Pelican* at Batavia Airport after a Christmas flight from the Netherlands. (Nationaal Archief)

Year	Miles Flown	Passengers	Freight (lbs)	Mail (lbs)
1928	37,450	2,110	7,910	458
1930	498,350	18,250	264,300	20,660
1934	594,370	17,630	164,700	60,770
1938	1,470,450	21,660	223,670	125,810
1940	1,480,456	21,300	314,160	143,920
1941	2,734,100	36,500	518,010	242,510
WAR				
1948	5,155,900	190,230	12,754,000	3,063,452
1949	6,128,478	267,320	18,972,500	4,398,615
Flights operated by newly established Garuda				
1950	6,407,900	298,600	19,825,652	4,000,508
1951	6,128,742	300,100	20,410,256	4,368,657

Source: Garuda Indonesia Airways NV, Amsterdam, Planning 1951–55.

Shortly after World War Two, the 19th Transport Squadron received the orders to start up regular flights within Indonesia. Civil aviation, however, is not the task of the military, and plans were made to set up a new airline.

When the war came close to an end, the cry for independence could be heard again in the kampongs and villages of the archipelago. On 17 August 1945, just two days after the Japanese capitulation, Koesno Sosrodihardjo Sukarno and Mohammad Hatta, two influential nationalist leaders, proclaimed Indonesian independence (limited to the islands of Java and Sumatra) and were appointed president and vice president. But this unilateral declaration was not accepted by the international community and certainly not by the Dutch government, which attempted to re-establish its rule. A bitter armed and diplomatic struggle would start. Sukarno had to move his revolutionary headquarters from Batavia to the villages surrounding Yogyakarta.

On 15 December 1946, the Liggadjati Agreement (named after the mountain village of the same name in West Java where the agreement was negotiated) was signed by representatives of the Netherlands and of the revolutionary government of Indonesia. With this agreement, the Netherlands clearly accepted the authority of the revolutionary government on the islands of Java, Sumatra and Madura (an island north of East Java). Areas on these islands, occupied by Dutch troops, would have to be turned over to the Republik. But some members of the Dutch parliament, which had to ratify the agreement, had objections and wanted to renegotiate it. On 20 July 1947, the representative of the Netherlands in Indonesia, Huib Van Mook, suddenly terminated the agreement. One day later, the Dutch military started Operation *Product*, a military offensive against areas of Java and Sumatra controlled by the Republic of Indonesia. This decision was motivated by the Dutch perception that the Republik had failed to curb the influence of Indonesian Chinese (who controlled a large part of the trade), Indonesian Indians and the rising of the Indonesian Communist Party. It would last from 21 July to 4 August 1947. Referred to by the Dutch as the first 'Politionele Actie', the Indonesians use the term 'Agresi Militer Belanda I' (Dutch Military Agression 1). During Operation *Product*, thousands of Indonesian civilians living in disputed areas were murdered by Dutch troops.

Indonesian resistance was fierce. A few days after the proclamation of the Indonesian independence by Sukarno and Hatta, they set up the Indonesian People's Security Bureau (Badan Keamanan Rakyat). The air division of this force was also formed, using Japanese aircraft scattered everywhere, especially on the islands of Java including the Bugis Air Base in Malang. The most numerous of these aeroplanes were the Yokosuka K5Y1 Willow (Cureng) trainers, which were hastily used to train newly recruited cadets. At the time of the founding, there was only one Indonesian citizen holding a multi-engine pilot licence from the pre-war Dutch Flying School. Agustinus Adisucipto was assisted by a few Japanese pilots who decided to stay in the newly born country, rather than return to their defeated homeland. On 9 April 1946, the Indonesian Air Force was officially formed. When Operation *Product* started, the Dutch destroyed most of the aircraft on the ground. Some aircraft, however, survived and were hidden in remote bases. On 29 July 1947, the first air operation by the newborn Air Force took place when three surviving Willows and a Mitsubishi Ki-51 Sonia conducted air raids at dawn on the Dutch army barracks in Semarang, Salatiga and Ambarawa, dropping incendiary bombs. From a tactical point of view, these raids did not have any effect on the Dutch positions, but psychologically it was a great success, as it proved that the Indonesian Air Force still existed. The Dutch had previously claimed they had destroyed the whole Air Force, and they never expected any attack from the sky. Although some Dutch Curtiss P-40E Warhawks tried to locate and destroy the 'guerilla' aircraft, they were not able to find them, as these aircraft, after a quick refuelling stop in Maguwo Air Base (now Yogjakarta Adisucipto International Airport), were hidden in remote areas.

In this way, the Indonesian Air Force could save a series of Mitsubishi A6M 'Zero-Sen', Aichi D3A 'Val' and Mitsubishi G4M 'Betty' aircraft.

Both Sukarno and Hatta realised that the small Indonesian Air Force alone would not be able to successfully fight the Dutch troops and break the blockade that the Dutch had set up to starve the population of areas that were under the control of the Republik. The effort to purchase transport aircraft started with the establishment of the Panitia Pusat Pengumpul Emas (Central Gold Collection Committee) by Hatta, Indonesia's first vice president, during a visit to Bukittingi in West Sumatra on 27 September 1947. The committee was led by A Karim, a director of the Bank Negara State Bank. The West Sumatra community collected 14kg of gold donations, which were used to buy a single Avro Anson in Thailand. The aircraft was previously owned by Paul H Keegan, an Australian citizen and former RAF pilot, and was registered VH-BBY. The aircraft was then flown by Keegan himself to the Gadut airfield in Bukittinggi. At the end of December 1947, Air Commodore Iswahyudi and Air Commodore Halim Perdanakusuma flew the aircraft (which was planned to be registered as RI-003) past the Dutch blockade to garner support from Singapore and Thailand. The two Indonesians then loaded military equipment and medicine in Songkla (Thailand). However, on their way home through Singapore, the aircraft crashed in Tanjung Hantu, killing both of its crew members. The aircraft pieces were scattered in the sea at Labuhan Bilik between Tanjung Hantu, Malaya and Teluk Senagih in North Sumatra. Perdanakusuma's body was found but Iswahyudi's was missing, although his wallet containing bank notes and cards with his name was found near the sea. The two men were later proclaimed national heroes. In order to honour them, a commemoration monument was erected in Bukittingi. Therefore, another Avro Anson (ex RAF AX 505) was bought from the RAF after Indonesia's independence was internationally recognised. On 20 June 1948, Sukarno travelled to Aceh (Sumatra) to start collecting funds, hoping he would be able to finance the purchase of some transport aircraft. As a result, within two days he collected the equivalent of 20kg in gold and 130,000 Singapore dollars. Sumatra had been selected as the target of propaganda for Dakota funds because its territory was a strategic propaganda area that enabled the establishment of trade relations with foreign countries. Apart from that, the natural wealth potential of this location enabled foreign currency to be earned by smuggling goods abroad. Smuggling was necessary, as the Dutch blockade made any legal export impossible.

Contributions came mainly from the 'Amai-Amai' of Sumatra (the Mothers of Sumatra). These ladies willingly provided jewellery and gold. Their husbands (rich traders) provided their contributions in Singapore dollars. Considering Sumatra is very close to Singapore, international trade was very important for the inhabitants of the island, and the Dutch blockade threatened to ruin them. So it is understandable that they decided to contribute to the war effort against the Dutch blockade. With the proceeds of this fundraising, Sukarno was able to purchase a second-hand Douglas Dakota in Hong Kong, which belonged to an American pilot, J H Maupin, and which was registered as VR.HEC. Upon arrival in Indonesia, the aircraft was re-registered as RI-001 (which is rather odd as the Avro Anson RI-003 was purchased prior to this Dakota RI-001). The aircraft was baptised *Seulawah*.

On 9 December 1948, the RI-001 was flown to Calcutta in India in order to arrange an overhaul of the engines. In this way, the aircraft escaped destruction by the Dutch, as, indeed, on 19 December, the second major military intervention under the codename 'Operatie Kraai' (Operation *Crow* or Agresi Militer Belanda II) started. By September 1948, the Dutch military command had succeeded in decoding the republic's encrypted secret code, gaining crucial information on Indonesian military and diplomatic strategies and plans. This enabled General Simon Hendrik Spoor to counteract republic actions on the battlefield and on the diplomatic stage. The Dutch were so confident of this advantage that they held a press conference in Jakarta three days prior to the actual attack. As a reaction, the Indian prime minister, Jawaharlal Nehru, offered to dispatch a private aircraft to fly Sukarno and

Monument for the Avro Anson RI-003. (Indonesian Ministry of Education and Culture)

Hatta from their headquarters in Yogjakarta to Bukittinggi in West Sumatra where they could then head an emergency government. A diplomatic delegation led by Sukarno would then be flown to New York via New Delhi to advocate for the republic's cause in the United Nations General Assembly. Throughout the Indonesian National Revolution, newly independent India had been sympathetic to the republic's cause, which they viewed as a struggle against Western imperialism. But Sukarno and Hatta refused this offer and chose to remain with their troops in Yogyakarta. On 19 December, Dutch aircraft took off from Bandung, heading for Yogyakarta. At the same time, major Indonesian centres in Java and Sumatra were attacked. After bombing the airport in Yogyakarta, Dutch paratroopers were dispatched to capture the radio station. In the late evening, the city of Yogyakarta had fallen into Dutch hands. Sukarno and Hatta were arrested by the Dutch and exiled to Bangka. A large proportion of the Indonesian independence fighters, however, were able to escape and made their way to Sumatra to join other republican forces. In the meantime, the emergency government in Sumatra managed to purchase more aircraft, which were used to smuggle arms into the country, whereas on their way to Singapore, they transported Indonesian exports.

Some of these aircraft were bought with the proceeds of fundraising in Sumatra, others were received as a gift from foreign pilots or leased from them. A Dakota RI-002 was one of the aircraft offered to the freedom fighters by Bobby Freeberg, an American pilot of Swedish origin. During the war, he had been flying over the Pacific to find Japanese ships hiding on the islands and destroying them. After the war, he remained in the Philippines where he set up a commercial company called CALI (Commercial Airlines Incorporation). It was there that he first met Petit Muharto Kartodirdjo, who worked for the Air Force of Sukarno. Just prior to the start of the second Dutch operation (Operation *Crow*), Freeberg leased his aircraft to the republican forces and flew to Yogjakarta. The aircraft was re-registered as RI-002. The aircraft flew different missions, including the dropping of specially trained Javanese troops in Kalimantan to assist Kalimantan freedom fighters. It also transported the first Indonesians to Rangoon (Burma) on their way to India where they were to train as pilots. On 29 September 1948, the RI-002 left Bukittingii with a cargo of gold to be used to finance the purchase of more aircraft. The flight plan was to fly from Yogjakarta to Gorda and then from there to Tanjung Karang and Bukittingi. Once the gold was loaded, the aircraft made its way to Sumatra but never arrived. It was only 30 years later, on 7 April 1978, that the wreckage of the aircraft was discovered in the jungle of Lampung by two poor farmers. Today, there is insufficient evidence to be able to prove conclusively what happened during the flight.

The RI-003 registration, which was originally that of the Avro Anson that crashed upon delivery, was later assigned to a Stinson L-5 acquired from Ralph Cobley, a former Royal Australian Air Force pilot, who flew in World War Two. RI-004 was another Avro Anson, also purchased with the donations from the people of Bukittinggi. This aircraft was purchased from Wade Palmer, a Scottish citizen, then flown by pilot Sudaryono and used for the delivery of goods and arms on routes within Sumatra. The aircraft was destroyed when the Maguwo Airfield was attacked by the Dutch during Operation *Crow*. Catalina RI-005 was originally an aircraft that also belonged to Ralph Cobley. The freedom fighters chartered the aircraft from Cobley after a meeting in Bangkok. In Indonesia, the aircraft obtained the registration RI-005. Cobley landed his aeroplane in Tulung Agung Lake in East Java. During 1948, the aircraft made different flights in Sumatra, using the many water bases available. The tasks carried out, among others, were to link the military command to the Sumatra command in Bukittinggi, as well as to transfer officers to and from Yogjakarta and to deliver medicine and food to villages struck by the Dutch blockade. It was, however, also rumoured that the aeroplane was used to transport opium in order to obtain foreign exchange that could be used to buy more aircraft. When, on 29 December 1948, the Dutch succeeded in occupying Jambi, the republican forces tried to move the aircraft to Singapore to prevent it from falling into Dutch hands. However, because of an engine problem that forced Cobley to take off with only one engine working, the aeroplane crashed into a barge on the Batanghari River. Both crew members died in the crash. Only much later, the wreckage was found and saved from the riverbed from a mud depth of 30 feet. Subsequently, the wreck was restored and can now be seen at the Jambi museum. Another Catalina, with registration RI-006, owned by Australian pilot James Fleming, was captured by the Dutch on 19 December 1948 and flown to Tjilitan, where it was transferred to Marine Vliegkamp Morokrembangan in Surabaya and subsequently stripped. It has to be noted that the prefix 'RI' (for Republik Indonesia) was never officially sanctioned by International Civil Aviation Organization, since Indonesia was not a truly independent state at that time.

While the fighting in Indonesia went on, the Dakota RI-001, which was in India for an engine overhaul, had been repaired. In order to prevent the Dutch from confiscating or destroying the aircraft, it was decided it would not immediately return to Indonesia. Instead, it was flown from India to Burma (now Myanmar). On the initiative of Air Officer Wiweko Supeno and with the assistance of the Indonesian representative in Burma, a commercial airline company under the name 'Indonesian Airways' was established on 26 January 1949, with its seat in Burma. At that time, there was a

The restored Catalina RI-005 in the Museum Perjuangan Rakyat Jambi. (Museum Perjuangan Rakyat Jambi)

Dutch paratroopers near the captured Catalina RI-006. (Hendrikse, Dutch National Archives)

rebellion in some regions, and the Burmese government was eager to charter the Dakota for military flights. These flights included the transportation of Burmese troops, weapons and ammunition. With the proceeds of these flights, the owners of Indonesian Airways could finance the training of Indonesian pilots in India and even the purchase of two more Dakotas (RI-007 and RI-009).

Obviously, the news of the second Dutch military operation (Operation *Crow*) had spread and became headline news in many countries around the world, which condemned the Dutch attacks in their editorials. As a result, the USA threatened to suspend Marshall Plan aid to the Netherlands. This aid included funds vital for the Dutch post-World War Two reconstruction efforts and had so far totalled $1bn. But instead of investing this money for the reconstruction of the Dutch economy, the Dutch government had spent almost half of it on funding their campaigns in Indonesia. Under American pressure, the UN Security Council called for the end of hostilities on 24 December 1948. In January 1949, it passed a resolution demanding the reinstatement of the republican government. Nevertheless, the guerilla war would continue for some time, until the signing of the Roem–Van Roijen Agreement on 7 May put an end to the hostilities. As a result of a series of Round Table conferences in 1949, the Netherlands granted independence to Indonesia (except Irian Jaya, which remained under Dutch control) on 27 December 1949. The United Nations not only ordered the Netherlands to give back all Dutch East Indies' wealth and resources to the government of the independent republic, but also ordered KLM Interinsulair Bedrijf to be returned to Indonesia. This company was one of the subsidiaries of KLM after taking over the privately owned KNILM.

Also in December 1949, there was a meeting between the Indonesian government and KLM regarding the start-up of a new national airline. President Sukarno decided the new airline should be

An historical picture of the RI-001. (IVAO Indonesia)

named 'Garuda Indonesian Airways'. Garuda is indeed the legendary Garuda bird, used by the god Vishnu on his many travels. During the Dutch–Indonesian Round Table Conference at The Hague, which took place from 23 August to 2 November 1949, Sukarno cited a Dutch poem written by a renowned Javanese scholar and poet, Raden Mas Noto Soeroto: 'I'm a Garuda, Vishnu's Bird, that spreads its wings high above the Islands'.

The first fleet of Garuda was inherited from KLM Interinsulair Bedrijf and not from Indonesian Airways in Burma that was owned by the AURI (Indonesian Air Force or Angkatan Udara Republik Indonesia). One day after the Netherlands acknowledged the sovereignty of the Indonesian Republic on 28 December 1949, two Dakota aircraft flew from Kemayoran Airport (Jakarta, formerly Batavia) to Yogjakarta to pick up Sukarno who became the first president of Indonesia. One year later, in 1950, Garuda Indonesia officially became a state-owned company.

After the recognition of sovereignty by the Dutch and the restoration of the power of the Indonesian government, organisational and personnel changes were made in the AURI. Based on the decision of the chief of staff of the Air Force, Indonesian Airways in Burma was liquidated and all activities were suspended. All Air Force personnel returned to Indonesia and joined other units of the AURI. The RI-001 Dakota arrived at Andir Air Base on 3 August 1950, after a flight from Rangoon via Bangkok to Medan. The aircraft was stationed at Andir Bandung Air Base.

Starting in the 1970s, the Angkatan Udara (Air Force) decided to repaint a series of surplus Dakotas into the original colour scheme of the RI-001. Afterwards, the aircraft were dispatched to several Indonesian islands where they serve as a monument to the first Indonesian pilots that fought for the independence of the country.

A former Angkatan Udara Dakota is being repainted in the colours of the first Dakota of Indonesian Airways. (Jozef Mols)

Above: This former Air Force Dakota is repainted in the old Garuda livery and serves as a monument. (Garuda Indonesia)

Left: President Sukarno arrives at Jakarta by DC-3. (Kemayoran Aviation Museum)

Chapter 2

Domestic and Regional Network

I ndonesian historians pretend that when Indonesian independence was acknowledged by the Dutch government, the Dakota *Seulawah*, with registration RI-001, was flown from Burma to Yogjakarta to pick up President Sukarno and Vice President Hatta and bring them to Jakarta. Of course, this fits within the nationalistic rhetoric of the 1950s. But the reality is different. RI-001 only returned to Indonesia in August 1950.

Coinciding with the Round Table conferences that culminated in the recognition of Indonesia's independence, the Indonesian government and KLM had negotiated the start-up of a new regional airline. It was agreed that KLM would take a 50 per cent stake in this new airline and would provide managerial and technical assistance.

The day after Indonesia's independence was internationally acknowledged, two KLM Dakotas, hastily repainted with the Garuda Indonesia Airways logo, colours and writing, were sent to Yogjakarta to pick up Sukarno, his family and the cabinet of the new government, and fly them to Jakarta, which became the new capital city of Indonesia. Therefore, 28 December 1949 is designated as the de facto date of birth of Garuda. But, oddly enough, the joint venture between KLM and the Indonesian government and the formation of Garuda was only based on the notary deed of Raden Kadiman number 137, dated 31 March 1950, which is therefore the legal date of birth of the new airline.

The notary deed, with document number 136, contains details of the transfer of assets to Garuda Indonesian Airways, including employee housing assets, operational vehicles, offices and, of course, a series of aircraft. They included 11 Douglas DC-3 passenger aircraft, 12 Douglas C-47 cargo aircraft and three PBY Catalina seaplanes. The Douglas DC-3 aircraft had registrations from PK-DPA to PK-DPK. The C-47 aircraft had a random registration number considering that the original was a grant from the Dutch military, especially from the 19 ML Transport Squadron. Based on this notarial deed, it also appears that Garuda received three PBY Catalina transport aircraft with PK-CTA, PK-CTB and PK-CTD registrations. Originally, the KLM Interinsulair Bedrijf had four Catalinas, but one of them had an accident during take-off and sank in Lake Poso in Central Sulawesi. Eventually, Garuda would have four Catalinas, as PK-CTE was handed over later as a replacement for the aircraft that was lost. Dr E Konijnenburg (previously director of KLM) would become the first president director of Garuda Indonesia and would serve until 1954, when he would be replaced by Ir. Soetoto till 1959. Four years after the start-up of Garuda, the airline was truly nationalised, and Indonesia became the only owner of the airline. As a token of gratitude towards the government of Burma for its assistance during the independence struggle, the Burmese government was presented with one DC-3 aircraft upon the formal incorporation of Garuda on 31 March 1950.

The original fleet, obtained through the agreement with KLM, was initially used on domestic services, linking the most important cities on the islands of Sumatra, Java and Sulawesi. But timetables from that period show that flights to Singapore and Penang (via Medan) and to Manila via Balikpapan were also introduced. On 23 September 1950, Garuda received its first Convair CV-240. In terms of technology, both the CV-240 and the Dakota still relied on radial piston engines. But the new aircraft was pressurised so that it could fly higher than the Dakota. It could also seat up to 40 passengers, whereas the capacity of the Dakota was restricted to only 20 people. Garuda would obtain a total of eight Convairs, which were flown over the Pacific Ocean via Hawaii, Guam and Wake Island until finally landing at Jakarta's Kemayoran Airport. The aircraft were registered PK-GCA to PK-GCI (minus PK-GCF). Obviously, it was a challenge to find pilots authorised to fly this new equipment, and Garuda had to rely on the KLM Assistance Group to train and provide such crews. The introduction of the new aircraft enabled Garuda to start-up flights as far away as Bangkok. Passengers originating in Indonesia could then connect in Thailand with flights by Pan Am, KLM and BOAC to reach other Asian and even European destinations.

In 1951, the Indonesian Ministry of Transportation decided to send young people to be trained to become Garuda pilots at the air training school at Hamble in the UK. It is no secret that offers for education always come with a price tag. Indonesia was supposed to buy British aircraft. In October 1953, Garuda ordered up to 14 units of the de Havilland Heron Type 1B, registered PK-GHA to PK-GHL. Garuda sent a total of 24 would-be pilots to the UK, but the group was finally split into two. The minimum licence to fly the Heron was SCPL (Senior Commercial Pilot's Licence) and the Hamble-1 group of pilots returned to Indonesia in March 1954. The rest of the group continued to attend courses until they got an ATPL (Airline Transport Pilot Licence), which allowed them to fly the Dakotas. However, in practice this division was not binding, as at that time a multi-type rating was applied, so ATPL holders could become Heron pilots and SCPL pilots could fly the Dakota (limited to domestic flights). After the orders for Convair CV-240s and Herons, Garuda ordered eight Convair CV-340s and three Convair CV-440 aircraft, each of which of the first ordered aircraft arrived in Indonesia in September 1950, April 1954 and January 1958. By 1959, Garuda's fleet comprised 20 Douglas DC-3/C-47 aircraft, eight Convair CV-240s, eight Convair CV-340s and three Convair

Convair CV-240 PK-GCC was delivered to Garuda on 7 September 1950 and left the fleet on 13 October 1964. On 20 October 1970, the aircraft returned to Indonesia with Mandala Seulawah Airlines as PK-RCO. (Thijs Postma collection)

Garuda used Convairs on its first Hajj pilgrimage flights. (Thijs Postma collection)

CV-440s alongside 14 de Havilland Herons. In addition to an extensive domestic network, the airline also offered flights to Singapore, Manila and Bangkok. And in 1956, Labuan in Malaysia was added as a stop on flights to Manila. As Indonesia has a large Muslim population, Garuda started operating flights to Mecca as of 1956. Convair aircraft were used on this pilgrimage route.

Sukarno had managed to obtain the independence of his country, but his appetite was still great, and his political actions would seriously influence the history of Garuda. While the Dutch East Indies had become fully independent in December 1949, the Dutch retained sovereignty over the western part of the island of New Guinea and took steps to prepare it for independence as a separate country. The Dutch and West Papuan leaders argued that the territory did not belong to Indonesia because the West Papuans were ethnically and geographically separated from Indonesians, had always been administered separately, and the West Papuans did not want to be under Indonesian control. Indonesia, on the other hand, tried to gain control of Western New Guinea (as the Dutch colony was called) through the United Nations. Starting in 1954, Indonesia sporadically launched military raids into Western New Guinea. Following the failure of negotiations at the United Nations, Sukarno escalated pressure on the Netherlands by nationalising Dutch-owned businesses and estates and repatriating Dutch nationals. Obviously, these actions increased tensions between Indonesia and the Netherlands and led to a sharp reduction in trade between the two countries. As a result, Garuda Indonesia Airways, which had been owned by the Indonesian government and KLM (each owned 50 per cent), was fully nationalised. The first CEO of the airline, the former KLM director, Konijnenburg, was replaced by an Indonesian citizen. But above all, the KLM Assistance Group, which had helped start up the Indonesian airline, was forced to leave the country. This in turn resulted in the sale of all Heron aircraft. Indeed, these aircraft had not been very popular, as they were used on shorter routes despite ticket prices being high. So Indonesians often took the train instead of a flight whenever they had to make short trips. Maintenance costs of the Herons were also high. Operating 14 units resulted in the maintenance of at least 56 Gipsy engines. While the Dakota and the Convair aircraft were all powered by Pratt & Whitney engines, the extra engine type caused an extra burden on the maintenance budget. Coupled with the drastic reduction in pilot numbers once the KLM Assistance Group had to leave the country, existing Garuda pilots were prioritised to fly Dakota and Convair aircraft. By 1960, there were no Herons left in Indonesia. Two of the aircraft had crashed while flying for Garuda, and the remaining aircraft were sold to C. Itoh & Company, a Japanese company that was originally engaged in the textile industry but after World War Two developed its business in the export-import sectors of oil and gas, heavy equipment, cars and aircraft. The company became the distributor of Heron aircraft to be operated by airlines serving domestic routes in Japan. Here these aircraft were very popular, as the fast bullet train we know nowadays did not exist yet.

Following a sustained period of harassment of Dutch diplomats in Indonesia, Sukarno formally severed ties with the Netherlands in August 1960. Indonesia also increased its military pressure on Dutch New Guinea by purchasing weapons from the Soviet Union and the Eastern Bloc. Over the following years, the Sukarno regime would become dependent on Soviet military support, but strangely enough, whereas Russian-made aircraft were purchased to serve in the Angkatan Udara, no Russian aircraft were bought by Garuda. It is clear the United States government feared growing communist influence in the country, especially as the Communist Party had received 16 per cent of the votes in the 1955 election. As the densely populated island of Java had been the administrative centre of the country, most of the natural resources could be found on other islands of the archipelago. This led to resentment and anti-Javanese feelings in many places. In 1957, this dissatisfaction with Java in general, and with Sukarno's policies in particular, had led to a bloodless coup on the islands of Sumatra and Sulawesi, where local military commanders took over the administration of their areas and set themselves up as virtual warlords. The United States tried to weaken the Sukarno regime by supporting the rebels. President Eisenhower asked CIA director Allen Dulles and his brother, Secretary of State John Dulles, to set up an instant air force to support the rebels. The plans received unofficial approval by the UK and Australia. Eastern European crews on the CIA payroll were used to limit direct American involvement to a minimum. Notwithstanding American assistance, the rebellion was crushed by the end of 1958.

On 19 December 1961, Sukarno decreed the establishment of the People's Triple Command or Tri Komando Rakyat (Trikora) in order to annex what Indonesia called West Irian by 1 January 1963. Trikora's operational command was to be called the Mandala Command for the Liberation of West Irian (Komando Mandala Pembebasan Irian Barat) with Major General Suharto (who would later become the second president of Indonesia) in command. In preparation for a planned invasion, the Mandala command began making incursions by land, sea and air into West Irian, confronting the Dutch over control of Western New Guinea. While the United States, the United Kingdom and Australia sided with the Netherlands' claims to Western New Guinea and were opposed to Indonesian expansionism, they were unwilling to commit military support to the Dutch. The Netherlands was unable to find sufficient international support for its New Guinea policy, as Sukarno was able to muster the support of the Soviet Union, the Warsaw Pact allies and the Non-Aligned Movement. In response to Indonesian claims, the Netherlands decided to speed up the process of implementing West Papuan self-rule under Dutch control from 1959 onwards. These measures included the establishment of a legislative New Guinea council in 1960, establishing hospitals, development of plantations and the creation of a Papuan Volunteer Corps to defend the territory. Also, the repair of former Japanese airfields and the construction of new airports became a necessity.

The United States did not support the surrender of West Irian to Indonesia, since the Bureau of European Affairs of the State Department considered it an act of trading one occupying power

A Garuda Convair 340. (Thijs Postma collection)

for another. However, in April 1961, Robert Komer and George Bundy began to prepare plans for the United Nations to give the impression that the surrender to Indonesia was legal. Although reluctantly, President John F Kennedy finally supported these plans, fearing that, without American support, the Indonesians would become further entrenched into the Soviet Bloc. The Netherlands finally gave way to American pressure and the threat of an attack on New Guinea by Indonesian forces, assisted by Soviet Bloc troops. On 15 August 1962, the Netherlands recognised Indonesia's resolve to take Western New Guinea and signed the New York Agreement, which handed over the former colony to an interim United Nations administration. The official handover to the United Nations Temporary Executive Authority took place on 1 October 1962. On 1 May 1963, Indonesia formally annexed Western New Guinea.

Immediately after World War Two and Indonesian independence, airline transportation in West Irian had been guaranteed by the Dutch MLD (Militaire Luchtvaartdienst or Military Aviation Service). Airports had been left by the Japanese after their surrender and were in very poor condition. Starting in 1950, KLM supplied one Dakota and some technicians under a 'time-charter' contract. In 1952, KLM took over all air transport within West Irian. By 1954, however, it became clear the region needed its own airline. C Mattern, appointed by KLM, got the order to study the possibility of setting up such a local airline. On 14 July 1955, the Nederlands Nieuw-Guinea Luchtvaart Maatschappij De Kroonduif (Dutch New Guinea Aviation Company De Kroonduif) was established with a seat in 's Gravenhage (The Hague) as a subsidiary of KLM. The airline started offering several routes throughout the territory with two de Havilland Canada Beavers. Later, the fleet was supplemented with Douglas DC-3 Dakotas and Scottish Aviation Twin Pioneers.

In the meantime, in Indonesia, the Garuda Dakotas and the Convair fleet were militarised during the *Trikora* campaigns. At least one Convair CV-240 was prepared to become a Garuda Wing Garuda command-post aircraft. But once the operation was over, and Indonesia took control of West Irian, the aircraft were returned. Garuda even inherited the aircraft, formerly used by De Kroonduif and could therefore expand its fleet with more Dakotas and a series of Scottish Aviation Twin Pioneers. A number of Kroonduif staff members decided to remain in Indonesia to assist Garuda in organising its network in West Irian, consisting of many flights to isolated communities in the dense forests.

Whereas, on the one hand, Garuda was confronted with the immense task of organising air transportation in a vast and difficult environment, it had once again had to face the fact some of its aircraft were transferred to the military. Indeed, encouraged by the success of his campaign in West Irian, Sukarno this time decided to start military operations in Kalimantan under the code name 'Operasi Dwikora'. The island of Kalimantan was shared by three countries. On the one hand, Malaysia had control over the former British Borneo in the west of the island. In the north, the Sultanate of Brunei was a British protectorate, whereas the southeastern part of the island was Indonesian territory. By a series of infiltrations, Indonesia tried to occupy and annex the Malaysian part of the island which, however, was supported by the British and Australians. Garuda's Convairs were used to transport troops and supplies to the Indonesian forces in Kalimantan and hence could not be used for civil air transportation on the other islands of the archipelago. In the end, Sukarno had to retreat from Kalimantan and soon after, in 1966, he was replaced by General Suharto, his former military leader during the campaign in West Irian. Sukarno was put under house arrest and died in 1970.

With the end of the Sukarno regime and the start of Suharto's 'New Order' policy (implemented with the help of American economists), Garuda entered a period of stability, which finally enabled the airline to draw up a map for future development.

A Garuda Convair CV-440 Metropolitan. (San Diego Air and Space Museum)

In exchange for pilot training in the UK, Garuda had to buy a series of de Havilland Herons. (Ed Coates collection)

Most of the Herons were sold to Japan. (Ed Coates collection)

Garuda's Scottish Aviation Twin Pioneer in Papua in the 1960s. (Ritter for United Nations Temporary Executive Authority)

The entire fleet of 'Kroonduif' was transferred to Garuda when Irian Jaya became part of Indonesia. (Thijs Postma collection)

Chapter 3
International Ambitions

Due to the policy of the Sukarno government and the resulting wars, Indonesia had become a rather isolated country. KLM had left the country in 1954 as well. Garuda had managed to set up international connections to Singapore and Bangkok, where passengers boarding in Indonesia could catch connecting flights to other destinations. But, of course, it was clear Garuda had international ambitions and wanted to further expand its own network. This required a modernisation of the fleet. By 1953, all Catalina aircraft had left the fleet. The Convair CV-240s would soon follow. In 1960, two aircraft (PK-GCD and PK-GCG) were sold to John Mecon in the USA. By 1962, three of them had crashed (PK-GCB, PK-GCE and PK-GCH)). In 1961, Garuda acquired three Lockheed L-188 Electra aircraft, which supplemented the remaining Convair fleet. These aircraft had nearly twice as many seats as the Convairs in Garuda's fleet and were powered by four Allison 501-D13 turboprops. Garuda put them to use on their flights from Jakarta via Singapore to Bangkok, but the new aircraft also offered the possibility of start-up flights on the Jakarta–Hong Kong–Tokyo route, as well as on the Jakarta–Manila–Hong Kong route. A direct flight from Jakarta to Hong Kong was inaugurated a few years later with the arrival of jet aircraft. Some Convairs were still used to fly the Medan to Kuala Lumpur route. All other Convair aircraft were now used on domestic services. The three remaining Convair CV-240s would be sold to the General Dynamics Corporation in 1964. Later, after being modernised as Convair CV-640s, they would return to Indonesia where they were used by Seulawah Airways.

Garuda's international expansion was very important, not only for the airline itself but also for the Indonesian government, which wanted to put the country on the map. To allow Garuda to focus on its international business development, the Indonesian government decided to set up a second state-owned airline that would operate domestic flights on 'thin' routes. Garuda would then be able to concentrate on major domestic routes and, of course, the international flights. This way, Merpati Nusantara Airlines was established in Jakarta on 6 September 1962. 'Merpati' is the Indonesian word for 'dove' whereas 'Nusantara' is a Javanese word found in the *Pararaton* (The Book of Kings), probably written in the 16th century. It means 'the outer islands' referring to the minor islands (the Indonesian archipelago minus Sumatra and Java). Merpati inherited part of the former Kroonduif fleet, including four de Havilland Otters and two Douglas DC-3 Dakotas, three Dornier DO-28s and six Pilatus Porter PC-6s. The company started up with a total of 583 staff members. By operating local flights, Merpati not only made it easier for Garuda to focus on connections between major cities (domestic) and international destinations, but also Merpati became a de facto feeder for Garuda as it transported passengers from the most remote areas of the archipelago to major cities like Jakarta, where passengers could book connecting flights to other important Indonesian cities or to foreign destinations.

After the arrival of the Electras, Garuda entered the jet age with three Convair 990s (PK-GJA, PK-GJB and PK-GJC). With this equipment, non-stop flights to Hong Kong could be started up, supplementing the Electra flights with a stop in Manila. The aircraft would, however, remain in the fleet for only a very short time. PK-GJA, delivered in 1964, crashed in Bombay in 1968. PK-GJB, which first served as a CV-990 demonstrator for Convair, was delivered to Garuda in October 1963 and sold to the California Airmotive Corporation in 1973. On its delivery flight to the USA, the aircraft crashed on the Jakarta–Guam leg on 10 September 1973. When in 1965, Indonesia re-established diplomatic relations with the Netherlands, Garuda started up its intercontinental services.

Convair jets were used on routes to Amsterdam, Frankfurt, Paris, Rome and Prague. On these flights, stops were made in Bangkok, Bombay and/or Cairo. Also a route to Phnom Penh was inaugurated. The reasons for the short period of time the Coronados remained in the fleet are many. Garuda estimated the aircraft were not adapted to the weather conditions in Indonesia and were difficult to maintain. Garuda had made a mistake when ordering the Convairs, but this is understandable. The airline had had very good experiences with the Convair propliners it had purchased earlier and supposed that the Convair jets would also perform to perfection. However, the '990' was a new type of aircraft and still had some teething problems. Also, Garuda had no previous experience with jets, which made the introduction of the Convair even more difficult. Instead of ordering more Convairs, the airline decided to obtain Douglas DC-8 jets, the first of which entered service in 1965 and was introduced on the European routes, but also on a Jakarta–Karachi–Athens route. In the 1960s and 1970s, Garuda would operate a total of 11 Douglas DC-8s in various series, the DC-8-55 being the most popular. The first of these aircraft was handed over in July 1966 (PK-GJD), the last one arrived in 1974. Garuda did not only operate this type on its regular network, but also leased DC-8 aircraft from other airlines. The pilgrimage flights to Mecca, started up in the 1950s, had become very popular as – thanks to the economic upturn – more Muslims were able to allow themselves this flight. On two occasions, however, the pilgrimage turned into disaster. On 4 December 1974, a Martinair DC-8 chartered to fly Indonesian pilgrims from Surabaya to Saudi Arabia crashed near Colombo in Sri Lanka killing 182 pilgrims, three flight attendants and eight crew members. Then, on 15 November 1978, an Icelandic DC-8, chartered by Garuda to bring pilgrims from South Kalimantan, crashed in Colombo. This tragedy killed 174 pilgrims while 75 survived. In subsequent years, Garuda refrained from making refuelling stops in Colombo, as larger aircraft such as the Douglas DC-10 and Boeing 747 could be used on non-stop flights to Mecca. Garuda did not only charter DC-8s from other airlines, but once in a while also leased out some of its own aircraft. A typical example is PK-GEA, delivered to Garuda as PK-GJD. Between 1969 and 1973, it was leased to KLM as PH-DCY. When the aircraft returned to Indonesia, it was registered PK-GEA.

This Lockheed Electra 188C crash landed in Manado on 16 February 1967, killing 22 of the 92 passengers. (Garuda Indonesia)

Two Convair jets waiting for passengers at the old Kemayoran Airport. (Jozef Mols collection)

Arrival of the first Garuda flight at Schiphol airport operated by a Convair Coronado. (Nationaal Archief Joost Evers for collectief Anefo)

In 1969, the stop in Cairo on flights to Europe was replaced by a stop in Beirut, and Garuda also added Sydney to its flight schedule, the first route to Australia. Besides expanding its international network, and hence buying modern jet equipment, Garuda obviously had to modernise its domestic fleet. Fokker F27-200s entered the fleet and replaced the ageing Convairs. The type would remain in service till 1975, when they were replaced by Fokker 28 Fellowships. Later on, starting in 1969, Garuda also took delivery of 12 Fokker F27-600s, which remained in service until 1977. The same year, the first of 24 Fokker F28-1000 jets entered the fleet (to be replaced by Fokker F28-3000s in 1982). In order to prepare for the introduction of the type, eight candidate pilots and two candidate co-pilots as well as an engineer were sent to Amsterdam to be trained by Fokker. The first Fokker F28 was flown from Schiphol (Amsterdam Airport) to Jakarta's Kemayoran Airport with stops in Tehran, Karachi, Calcutta and Bangkok, arriving in Jakarta on 11 August 1971. Before starting commercial operations, the aircraft was taken on a five-day test-and-presentation tour around Indonesia, landing at all airports in major cities. In 1973, seven more Dutch jets – this time the Fokker F28 – would enter the fleet, followed by an unknown number of Fokker F28-4000s in 1978. With a total of 62 F28s in service, Garuda was holding the title for the largest operator of the type in the world. Of course, Garuda did not buy that many Fokker aircraft, because the F28-3000 series was purchased through the trade-in with the MK-1000, so that the total number of aircraft purchased was 34 units. Nevertheless, many claim the Fokker-28 fleet was the backbone of Garuda's domestic and regional network.

Nearly at the same time as the Fokker F28, the first of the (somewhat larger) Douglas DC-9-30s also entered the fleet. Whereas the Fokker F28 was used on most of the domestic routes, the DC-9 could operate flights between the largest cities where more passengers could board the aircraft. Garuda would operate a total of 25 DC-9s. The last one left the fleet in 1993. The type was replaced by the Boeing 737 Classic, just like the Fokker F28s.

Whereas Garuda was rapidly expanding, it was no longer the only airline company in Indonesia. Of course, there was Merpati Nusantara Airlines, owned by the government, but this airline was an important feeder for Garuda. However, in 1968, Sempati Air was established. At that time, the new airline limited its operations to charter flights for oil companies but would later become a fierce competitor. And in 1970, Mandala Airlines started up its operations, though at that time it was not yet a major competitor for Garuda. Nevertheless, the emergence of private airlines would become a headache for the Garuda management some years later.

The expansion of its international network also forced Garuda to purchase some larger jets, as passenger numbers continued to increase. In 1976, the airline took delivery of its first Douglas DC-10-30, giving it the capability to carry more passengers and fly longer flights. The type would replace the Douglas DC-8 and Convair 990 fleet on routes within Asia and to Europe. Garuda would use a total of 26 of these aircraft between 1976 and 2005, when the model was replaced by Airbus A330 jets. The Douglas DC-10 would become an integral part of the Garuda fleet for the years to come and would also be used on Hajj pilgrimage flights, including one Douglas DC-10-10 leased from Key Airlines. For this occasion, several DC-10s would be leased to supplement Garuda's own fleet during the busy months of Ramadan. In 1980, the fleet DC-10s would be complemented with Garuda's first Boeing 747-200 aircraft on high capacity or long-range routes like the Jakarta–Hong Kong, Jakarta–Perth, Melbourne–Sydney–Denpasar–Jakarta or Jakarta–Amsterdam (via Anchorage) routes.

The large-scale revitalisation of the airline and its remarkable expansion prompted Garuda to develop comprehensive training programmes for its air and groundcrews. Therefore, a dedicated training facility was established in West Jakarta under the name Garuda Indonesia Training Center.

Garuda's growth did not mean all staff members were happy. Many complained about low wages (compared to other international airlines), lack of social security benefits or mediocre housing allowances. On 29 January 1980, some 120 Garuda pilots went on strike. The strike action was the climax and demanded that Garuda management improved the payroll system and welfare of its cockpit crews. Carrying out a strike in the New Order era was an act of courage in itself, especially since President Suharto's government considered strikes as a violation of law and even a subversive action against the legal government. Pilots therefore risked being sentenced to jail. As a result of the crisis, domestic routes were disrupted because the majority of pilots on strike were Fokker F28 and Douglas DC-9 pilots. Many passengers were rebooked on flights operated by Merpati, Bouraq and Mandala. But also military and civilian agencies immediately took action. The commander of Kopkamtib (Operational Command for Restoring Security and Order), Admiral Soedomo, assigned the Air Force chief of staff, Marshal Ashadi Tjahjadi, to take over the routes left by Garuda. The Air Force immediately deployed its transport aircraft, including four Fokker F27s and four Lockheed C-130 Hercules. This air bridge continued to operate under the rules of civil aviation, although the 'A' markers of the Air Force were changed to 'PK' registration numbers of the civil fleet. Ticket prices and meals on board were the same, but, of course, passengers did not enjoy the same levels of comfort, as they were crammed into transport aircraft designed to carry troops and cargo. All Air Force aircraft arrived at Jakarta's Kemayoran Airport two days after the outbreak of the strike and immediately started providing service routes to cities in Java, Sumatra and Sulawesi. The operation was very remarkable and efficient, as about 70 per cent of the average number of passengers could be transported. After the strike was broken by the action of the military, Garuda pilots apologised to the public and returned to work on 3 February 1980. Gradually, the military aircraft could return to their bases.

Besides these first social actions in Indonesia, where trade unions (still underground) started to gain influence among the airline crews, Garuda also played its part in a series of hijackings and bombings. On 28 March 1981, a McDonnell Douglas DC-9 took off from Kemayoran Airport in Jakarta on a flight to Polonia International Airport in Medan (North Sumatra). After take-off, five hijackers stood up from their seats. Some pointed their guns at the pilot, while others patrolled

A Garuda Douglas DC-8-55 PK-GEA. (Thijs Postma collection)

A Garuda Douglas DC-8-55 PK-GJD. (Thijs Postma collection)

the aisle, monitoring passengers. They demanded the pilot fly to Colombo in Sri Lanka, but as the aircraft did not have enough fuel, a stop was made at Penang International Airport in Bayan Lepas (Malaysia). During this stop, one elderly lady, who was crying all the time, was released. After refuelling, the aircraft took off and landed at Don Mueang Airport in Bangkok where the hijackers read out their demands. The primary demand was the release of 80 individuals, recently imprisoned in Indonesia following the 'Cicendo Event' two weeks earlier, where Islamists attacked a police station in the Cicendo sub-district of Bandung (Java). Furthermore, the hijackers demanded the sum of $1.5m, as well as another aircraft to fly them to Sri Lanka. Furthermore, they asked that the Indonesian government would deport all Israeli citizens from the archipelago. The hijackers told the Thai police to deliver their demands to the Indonesian government and threatened to blow up the aircraft with all passengers aboard if their demands were not met. After a crisis meeting, the Indonesian government ordered the deputy commander of the Armed Forces to conduct a counter-terrorist raid to rescue the hostages. A Douglas DC-9, borrowed from Garuda and similar to the hijacked aircraft, was used for three days by the newly established Kopasandha (Indonesian Special Forces) to rehearse a raid. Then, the team of commandos set off for Bangkok on board a Garuda Douglas DC-10. On 31 March 1981, the team was ready to intervene, but the Thai government did not give permission for Indonesian forces to take over the aircraft, as it was on Thai territory. In desperation, the Indonesian strategic intelligence chief, Benny Mourdani, contacted the CIA station in Bangkok. American assistance was hoped for, as many of the passengers aboard the hijacked aeroplane were American citizens. Under American pressure, the Thai government finally authorised an Indonesian raid as the aircraft involved was registered in Indonesia and most passengers were Indonesian citizens, provided it would be assisted by the Royal Thai Air Force Security Force Regiment. The Garuda aeroplane was stormed by Indonesian troops, surprising the hijackers. Three of them were killed. Unfortunately, one Indonesian soldier and Captain Herman Rante, the pilot of the aircraft were also killed by 'friendly fire'. Two of the hijackers surrendered, whereas all the

A Garuda Fokker F27 Friendship at Halim Perdana Kusumah Airport. (Jozef Mols)

A Garuda Fokker F28-4000. This picture was published in an old Garuda in-flight magazine. (Garuda Indonesia)

passengers were saved. A third hijacker managed to leave the aircraft with a grenade in his hand, but he was shot before he could throw it. The Indonesian military team took the surviving hijackers back to Indonesia on board the Garuda Douglas DC-10, but they were killed on the way home – probably as vengeance for the death of one comrade and the pilot of the hijacked aeroplane.

This Fokker F28-1000 was delivered to Garuda in 1974 and remained in the fleet until 1985. (Tom Zethof)

This Douglas DC-9-32 was sold to the Philippines in 1995. (Jozef Mols collection)

A Douglas DC-9 in the new livery of Garuda. (Jozef Mols)

The Douglas DC-10-30 was delivered in October 1977. (Tom Zethof)

This Boeing 747-200 was delivered to Garuda in August 1980. (Tom Zethof)

An aerial view of Soekarno Hatta Airport. (Gunawan Kartapranata)

Chapter 4

Challenges and Problems

On 21 June 1982, Garuda became the launch customer of the Airbus A300B4-220FFCC (forward facing crew cockpit), which was the first variant of the A300 capable of being operated with two pilots instead of three. By 1984, nine of these were in service. (They would be replaced by Airbus A330s in 1999.) They were supplemented by a fleet consisting of eight Douglas DC-10s, 24 Douglas DC-9s, 45 Fokker F28s and six Boeing 747-200s. In 1985, Garuda's CEO, Reyn Altin Johannes Lumenta, who had been CEO for just one year, made the controversial decision to hire foreign consultants Landor Associates to create a new logo, livery and brand for the airline, a project that at the time was regarded as expensive and unnecessary. However, later on, this move was applauded as vital for the reputation and corporate identity of Garuda Indonesia as the national airline.

Although outsiders could have the impression that Garuda was a company with a healthy growth path, this was not entirely the case. Underneath, the airline had a lot of problems. The pilot strike in 1980 had only been the first warning of more trouble ahead. First of all, the airline was misused by politicians for personal ambitions and profits. Friends of President Suharto were appointed to the board of directors, even if they had no management or business experience. At one time, Garuda had more vice presidents than it had aircraft in its fleet. The modern headquarters of Garuda, close to the political heart of Indonesia, was manned by hundreds of high-level managers and their retinue. Nobody was aware of their exact functions and nobody cared. Furthermore, Garuda was also an instrument of domestic policy. Uniting the large population, spread over thousands of islands in the archipelago, was a big challenge for President Suharto. Communication was needed to create a nation. Hence, Garuda had the task of connecting even the least populated areas with major cities in Indonesia. The profitability of the complex network that resulted was of less importance; ticket prices had to remain low, considering the fact that the average yearly income of Indonesian citizens was only $600! Only the happy few could afford air travel, and, of course, the aircraft were often used by government officials, their families and friends to travel between the islands and to nearby destinations – all free of charge!

The Airbus A300-600 was Garuda's first aircraft type with a two-man crew. PK-GAL entered the fleet in 1991 and was sold to Ansett in 1997. (Jozef Mols)

Airbus A300-600 PK-GAO entered the fleet in 1992 and was sold to Ansett in 1997. (Jozef Mols)

Garuda introduced the McDonnell Douglas MD-11 to supplement its DC-10 fleet. (Jozef Mols)

This Douglas DC-10-30 was added to the fleet in 1979 and stored at Jakarta Soekarno-Hatta Airport in 2004. (Jozef Mols)

Not only Garuda but also Merpati experienced the negative influence of this political situation, and soon, Garuda had to take over Merpati to avoid the domestic carrier going bankrupt. (In fact, Garuda had already taken over Merpati in 1978, but this remained rather a 'token' takeover.) Merpati was integrated into Garuda's bookkeeping in 1989, but it continued to operate under its own brand name. While Garuda and Merpati were supposed to remain competitive, thanks to their both offering jet services on the domestic network, soon other private airlines started up competing routes. Bouraq and Mandala managed to obtain Boeing 737s for use on their domestic flights. They not only offered domestic flights but also opened regional routes. Bouraq started up flights to Japan and the Philippines. But the strongest competition came from Sempati Air. The airline was originally established to fly charter flights for the Indonesian oil industry. But whereas President Suharto wanted Garuda and Merpati to promote the unity of the country, his son had started up Sempati Air as a 'cash-cow'. Revenue generated from ticket sales was used to finance long-term projects in the fields of hotel construction and real estate. This was only possible thanks to 'creative management'. Aircraft were refuelled at air force installations (the fuel was never paid for); catering companies had to wait more than two years to have their invoices paid, and the insurance contributions, paid by foreign pilots, never reached the insurance company but disappeared into the pockets of Tommy 'Bangbang' Suharto (which became clear when a few houses of foreign pilots burned down). Whereas gambling was strictly forbidden in Indonesia, the Sempati gang set up a casino on nearby Christmas Island (an Australian territory). Also, of course,

Sempati would fly thousands of gamblers from Indonesia to the Sempati-owned casino on Australia's Christmas Island. But thanks to this criminal management, the airline could offer an outstanding service that was often much better than the standards offered by Garuda. While Garuda passengers had to face traffic jams in order to go to the airport or to the Garuda terminal in downtown Jakarta (and then travel by bus to the airport), Sempati passengers were offered a free taxi ride from their home straight to the airport. Sempati VIP lounges were state of the art. And the airline could sponsor cultural and sports events – something Garuda had never done. When Sempati also started offering regional flights to Singapore, Kuala Lumpur, Taipeh and Australia, Garuda and Merpati came under even more pressure. By 1993, the consolidated loss of Merpati in Garuda's bookkeeping amounted to more than $11.97m. Garuda itself was soon dragged into a price war with Sempati and other competitors. Although the Indonesian Ministry of Transportation did not allow ticket price discounting, creative managers did find, once again, some solutions. The prohibition was only valid within the Indonesian territory. Therefore, they validated ticket stocks at their foreign sales offices in Singapore or Australia and sold them afterwards with a huge discount (up to 30 per cent) in the Indonesian market. Garuda's turnover on domestic routes (40 per cent of its total turnover) had decreased by 7.78 per cent by 1993. But there was also foreign competition. In order to stimulate tourism (the fourth most important economic sector after oil, timber and textiles), the Minister for Tourism, Joop Ave, advocated the introduction of an 'Open Sky' policy, allowing foreign airlines to start up flights to a series of Indonesian holiday destinations. More than 60 per cent of all tourists at that time originated in Asian countries, and it was hoped the limited Open Sky policy would result in lower ticket prices and hence stimulate the tourism industry. Of course, Garuda had to follow by lowering its own fares on Asian routes, resulting in less profit or even some loss of revenue on these routes. Due to the creation of the Association of Southeast Asian Nations (ASEAN) free-trade organisation, airlines in member states got the right to start up flights to Indonesia, not limited to Jakarta but also including major airports like Surabaya, Yogjakarta, Denpasar, Manado, Medan, Padang, Ujung Padang and Lombok. The consequences for Garuda were not only limited to the fact it lost passengers on regional flights, but also on domestic routes, as, indeed, feeder services from and to Jakarta were no longer necessary, as many airports opened immigration services to handle foreign (Asian) tourists arriving on Asian carriers. Furthermore, the foreign carriers that had opened routes to Indonesian cities also offered international connections in their own hubs in their home countries, further eroding the market position of Garuda. Garuda, which had enjoyed a protected position for years, thanks to the protectionist government policy, was no longer able to adapt to the new market situation. Between 1990 and 1994, the total number of passengers transported by Garuda decreased by more than 20 per cent.

Notwithstanding its problems, Garuda went on with the modernisation of its fleet. In 1991, the airline took delivery of its first Douglas MD-11s, which would gradually replace the DC-10 on flights to Europe and also enabled the airline to launch services to Los Angeles via Honolulu. Garuda also obtained Boeing 737-300 equipment and would use a total of 29 of these aircraft, the last of which was phased out in 2014. In 1993, Boeing 737-400 jets joined the fleet, which would remain in service till 2012. In 1994, the first Boeing 747-400 was delivered. The type would soon become the mainstay of the Garuda fleet until 2015, operating Hajj pilgrimage flights and high-density, short-haul routes.

Hajj pilgrimage flights became so important that the airline had to take special precautions. After the closure of the Kemayoran Airport, Garuda had moved to the new Soekarno-Hatta Airport in Jakarta. The number of Hajj passengers increased year after year as a result of the growing Indonesian economy. On some days, the airport was overcrowded by passengers of such flights as the Hajj flights had to take place during a compressed two-month period dictated by the Muslim calendar. As many of them came from faraway islands in the archipelago and had no flying or travelling experience, the situation was

This Boeing 747-200 was delivered in 1980 when the fleet was modernised. (Tom Zethof)

New Boeing 737-300s joined the fleet. PK-GWA was damaged beyond repair on 16 January 2002. (Jozef Mols)

A Boeing 737-300 at Denpasar (Bali) Airport. (Jozef Mols)

Boeing 737-300 PK-GGN, with the logo for the 50th anniversary of Garuda, was later transferred to low-cost subsidiary Citilink. (Jozef Mols).

sometimes 'confused', with people sleeping in the corridors and on the staircases, making fires to make tea in the morning and cooking rice in the afternoon. Therefore, the military made available part of the Halim Perdanakusuma Airport to the east of Jakarta and built a tented camp to accommodate the pilgrims. Although these flights to Mecca were challenging, they were also lucrative. It is estimated as much as ten per cent of the company's annual revenues stemmed from pilgrimage flights. The challenge for Garuda was to maintain its regular services on established routes and at the same time meet the demands of the inflexible Hajj flight schedule. Scheduled as frequently as every hour, outbound flights (often by leased aircraft, flown by foreign crews) were full on departure and empty on the return leg. After the pilgrimage, the pattern was reversed. In the period between 1980 and 1990, Garuda transported an estimated 80,000 Hajj passengers per year.

In order to cope with the fleet modernisation, Garuda opened its own aircraft maintenance centre at the Soekarno-Hatta Airport in Jakarta. Due to the expanding fleet, Garuda now was placed among the 30 largest airlines in the world. With a fleet of 75 of its own aircraft, supplemented by several others leased to meet route demands, Garuda expanded its service to include 16 domestic destinations. Other loss-making routes were transferred to the Merpati subsidiary. In order to allow Merpati to operate these flights, Garuda would also transfer some older aircraft (including Fokker F28s and Douglas DC-9s) from its fleet to the Merpati fleet. Furthermore, the Garuda flight schedule included 37 international cities on five continents. Market research for Garuda indicated that European travel to Indonesia was likely to increase six-fold by the year 2000. In a sales mission led by the new Garuda president Wage Mulyono (appointed in January 1992), Garuda explored European options and added Münich to its list of destinations. According to the airline's research and independent research by the Atma Jaya Catholic University in Jakarta, Germany represented one of Indonesia's highest-yield markets for tourism. Over 20 per cent of Germany's trade volume with the ASEAN was absorbed by Indonesia, and Germany ranked second behind only the United Kingdom in visitor arrivals to Indonesia. By adding a second German destination to its schedule (Frankfurt was established in 1965), Garuda predicted that Germany would eventually become the single largest source of tourists to Indonesia. Future plans included expansion of the route network to include Houston, Montreal and Vancouver.

In order to support the tourism promotion, initiated by Joop Ave, Garuda sponsored the 'Visit Indonesia 1991' campaign and even set up a subsidiary engaged in the management of Indonesian hotels. In 1994, the Aerowisata head office was moved to the Soekarno-Hatta Airport in order to perform catering services for Garuda and other international airlines.

If the early 1990s were not easy on Garuda and Merpati, the late 1990s would become even more turbulent and difficult. First of all, two separate accidents seriously damaged the reputation of the airline. On 13 June 1996, a Denpasar-bound Garuda McDonnell Douglas DC-10-30 overran the runway at Fukuoka Airport in Japan upon departure. Investigations revealed pilot error and bad maintenance. And on 26 September 1997, an Airbus A300 flying from Jakarta to Medan crashed 18 miles short of Medan, killing all 234 people on board. But 1997 was also the start of the great Asian Financial Crisis. The crisis started in Thailand on 2 July 1997, when the Thai baht collapsed after the Thai government was forced to float the baht owing to lack of foreign currency to support its currency peg to the US dollar. Capital flight ensued almost immediately, beginning an international chain reaction. Besides Thailand, Indonesia and South Korea were the countries most affected by the crisis. As the crisis spread, most of the Southeast Asian countries and Japan saw slumping currencies, devalued stock markets and other asset prices and a precipitous rise in private debt. Although most of the governments of Asia had seemingly sound fiscal policies, the International Monetary Fund stepped in to initiate a programme to stabilise the currencies of South Korea, Thailand and Indonesia. The efforts to stem a global economic crisis, however, did little to stabilise the domestic situation in Indonesia. After 30 years in power, Indonesian President Suharto was forced to step down on 21 May 1998 in the wake of widespread rioting that followed sharp price increases caused by a drastic devaluation of the rupiah. Over the year, the rupiah had lost 75 per cent of its purchasing power. The middle classes, who had always been supported by Suharto, saw their recently acquired wealth disappear and they turned against the president. The effects of the crisis would linger on well into the new century. For Garuda and Merpati, the economic crisis resulted in higher fuel prices, as these had to be paid for in US dollars. This resulted in a drastic reduction in operations, mainly within the Asian region, but also on the intercontinental network. European operations were scaled back, but due to historical links with the Netherlands, flights to Amsterdam continued as well as operations to Frankfurt and London.

The crisis, which obviously had serious financial consequences for Garuda and Merpati, nevertheless had some positive outcomes as well. Garuda CEO Wage Mulyono (in charge since 1992) had made it clear he wanted to drastically reform the airline. Flight schedules had been adapted and loss-making routes had been suspended. Mulyono also wanted to modernise the fleet. In 1994, it became known the airline had ordered six Boeing 777s. The fleet renewal, however, was very expensive, and Garuda ended up with enormous debts. For President Suharto there was only one possibility: the airline had to be privatised. At that time, however, the Jakarta stock exchange was still very small with its total market capitalisation at only $35bn. Besides, the balance sheets of Garuda had to be 'cleaned' before a public offering could be considered. The Asian Financial Crisis made it impossible to introduce Garuda shares on the Jakarta stock exchange. But Mulyono had another idea. By buying new aircraft, Garuda could sell off older models like the Fokker F28 and Douglas DC-9. However, President Suharto did not agree with this policy, and the sale of aircraft was even forbidden unless they were to be sold to one of three Indonesian companies: PT Arthaska Nusaphala, PT Sakanusa Dirgantara or KFS Aviation Inc. Needless to say that these three companies belonged to either Tommy Suharto or to other 'friends' of the Suharto family. For the sale of eight Fokker F28s to a 'friend' of Suharto, Garuda only received $2.7m. Later on, this 'friend' of the President rented the aircraft to Merpati at a price of $950 per flight hour. The same trick was used when Garuda wanted to sell a series of older Airbus A300s. The airline could obtain $9m per unit, but it was forced by Suharto to sell the aircraft for a total of $43m. Disgusted by the corruption of Suharto and his gang, Mulyono resigned in 1995. The Indonesian government started negotiations with KLM, hoping this Dutch airline would invest fresh capital in the ailing Indonesian company, but owing to the Asian Financial Crisis, tourism and business in the area had decreased in such a way that an investment in the region would not have been a wise idea for KLM.

Boeing 737-400s like this one with the 'Visit Indonesia' logo were introduced on domestic and regional routes. (Jozef Mols)

Boeing 747-400s were used on European routes. (Jozef Mols)

Garuda had to lease aircraft for its Hajj pilgrimage flights. Due to lack of time, this Tower Air 747-200 was not fully repainted. (Jozef Mols)

This American 747-200 was leased for Hajj pilgrimage flights. (Jozef Mols)

Also, Malaysian 747-200s were leased for the pilgrimage season. (Jozef Mols)

Merpati became a Garuda subsidiary and feeder, using Fokker props on short-haul flights. (Jozef Mols)

This Fokker F28-4000 was part of Garuda's fleet as PK-GKJ until it was transferred to Merpati in 1996 and registered as PK-MGL. (Jozef Mols)

In 1994, Merpati leased this Douglas DC-9-32 from Garuda. (Jozef Mols)

On its short-haul routes, Garuda subsidiary Merpati also used the BAe ATP 72. (Jozef Mols)

Merpati had many Casa CN235-10s in its domestic fleet, feeding passengers for Garuda. (Jozef Mols)

On dense domestic routes, Garuda feeder Merpati used Boeing 737-200 equipment. (Jozef Mols)

The BAe 146-100 was an unlikely bird in the Merpati fleet. (Jozef Mols)

Merpati purchased a series of Avic Ark 600 aircraft for its feeder services. (AVIC)

Garuda's new maintenance hall at Jakarta Soekarno-Hatta Airport. (Jozef Mols collection)

Merpati jets at the Garuda maintenance facility in Jakarta. (Jozef Mols)

Also, military aircraft like this one from the Indonesian Navy are maintained by Garuda. (Jozef Mols)

Sempati became Garuda's main competitor. (Jozef Mols)

Mandala was competing with Garuda on both domestic and regional routes. (Jozef Mols)

Bouraq also started competing with Garuda. (Jozef Mols)

Lion Air started up as a small low-cost airline but soon became one of the largest airlines in Indonesia and Garuda's strongest competitor. (Jozef Mols)

Garuda's maintenance facility at Jakarta Airport was regularly modernised. (Jozef Mols collection)

Garuda's maintenance facility at Jakarta Airport. (Jozef Mols collection)

A Boeing 737 Max 8 waits its turn to be serviced at the maintenance facility. (Jozef Mols collection)

Chapter 5

The European Ban

The departure of President Suharto did not immediately change the business climate in Indonesia, as the roots of corruption still had to be eradicated, which took some time. However, the advantage for Garuda was the fact that Tommy Suharto lost his presidential protection from his father, and now creditors dared to start action in court against him in order to claim the payment of outstanding invoices. As a result, Sempati Air – Garuda's main domestic competitor – had to cease all international flights. On domestic flights, a mixed crew consisting of a foreign pilot and an Indonesian co-pilot was introduced. This was necessary to avoid an underpaid Indonesian pilot being bribed into flying his aircraft outside Indonesia so that the aircraft could be impounded by creditors. Another advantage was that Garuda's management was now free to execute decisions made earlier by former CEO Mulyono. The loss-making Merpati subsidiary was put under the jurisdiction of the Ministry for Transportation on 29 April 1997. Garuda only kept a nine per cent share in the carrier. Foreign consultants did a series of audits and arranged for a debt restructuring for Garuda. Some creditors were even willing to exchange their claims for Garuda shares. As a result, the balance sheet, which was $160m in the red in 1998, ended with a positive figure of $120m in 2001. The 1999 profit was the first for Garuda in a decade. Garuda began to reopen some of the 17 international routes that had been closed in the wake of the Asian Financial Crisis and secured a leasing deal for seven Boeing 737-800s to replace lost capacity. All these positive results were the basis for increased awareness among employees concerning the importance of service to customers and, most importantly, revitalised the Garuda Indonesia spirit. All of a sudden, the on-time performance of Garuda improved and many tourists even ranked Garuda 'the overall best domestic airline' among Indonesian carriers, according to a study performed by the Universitas Atma Jaya in Jakarta. Nevertheless, there was still room for improvement, as the same survey indicated that 16.83 per cent of the respondents considered the service level of all domestic airlines together as 'poor', 9.9 per cent considered them to be 'average', whereas 37.62 per cent rated them as 'good' and 15.85 per cent as 'very good'. These are important figures, as 69.36 per cent of foreign visitors to Indonesia used domestic airline transportation during their holiday.

In an effort to cope with domestic competition, Garuda established its own low-cost subsidiary, Citilink, in 2001. Operations commenced on 16 July of that year with two Fokker F28 Fellowhips transferred from the mainline fleet. By the end of 2001, Garuda had transferred five F28s to Citilink. By 2004, the airline was serving ten domestic destinations, and Garuda began to replace the Fokker F28s with Boeing 737-300s.

This, however, does not mean there was room for euphoria. The outlook for international air travel was exacerbated by the terrorist attacks in New York on 11 September 2001, which caused a major drop in travel and tourism on a worldwide scale. According to the Association of Asia Pacific Airlines, the number of passengers decreased by 8.1 per cent in the aftermath of the attacks. However, Garuda was able to hold on to profitability and posted a profit of $60m. Nevertheless, although plans for privatisation were still alive, they were deferred until 2003. On 12 October 2002, two bombs ripped through the Kuta area of the Indonesian tourist island of Bali, leaving 202 people dead. Among those killed at Paddy's Irish Bar and the nearby Sari Club were people from 21 countries, including 88 Australians, 38 Indonesians and 28 Britons. Bali was chosen by the Southeast Asian militant network,

Jemaah Islamiah Riduan Isamuddin, also known as Hambali, as Bali was 'frequented by Americans and their associates', according to Ali Imron who was jailed for life in 2003 for his part in the attacks. If the New York attacks had an immediate worldwide impact, the impact of the Bali bombings especially affected Indonesian tourism. In 2003, SARS (severe acute respiratory syndrome) spread throughout Asia. The first cases were recorded in the Chinese province of Guangdong by the end of 2002, and the disease rapidly spread to Vietnam. Ultimately, the epidemic affected 26 countries and resulted in more than 8,000 cases in 2003. The SARS coronavirus (SARS-CoV) was identified in 2003. It causes an atypical pneumonia and results in the death of about 15 per cent of patients. The virus is an animal virus from an as-yet-uncertain animal reservoir, perhaps bats, that spreads to other animals (civet cats, a delicacy in China). The outbreak resulted in a dramatic drop in tourism and travel, mainly in the Southeast Asian region. The economic growth in China even came to a complete standstill for some time. In preparation for a privatisation of the airline in 2003, Garuda announced plans to spin off its maintenance business with 2,750 related employees, as well as other non-core units. After a couple of years of promising recovery from the Asian Financial Crisis, Garuda ran at a loss in the first half of 2003. And although Garuda still controlled about 50 per cent of the domestic market, its operating margins had been cut in half. After the forced departure of President Suharto, the government had indeed decided to deregulate the aviation market, resulting in the creation of nearly three dozen 'bare bones' domestic airlines. In order to strengthen its position, Garuda began a marketing arrangement with Malaysian Airline Systems that effectively established Kuala Lumpur as an external hub for Garuda's long-haul international operations.

The ordeal had not yet come to an end for Indonesia and Garuda. On 26 December 2004, a major undersea earthquake occurred. It had a magnitude of 9.1 with the epicentre off the westcoast of northern Sumatra. As a result, a series of massive tsunami waves grew up to 100 feet once heading inland. Communities along the surrounding coasts of the Indian Ocean were severely affected, and the tsunamis killed an estimated 227,898 people in 14 countries, making it one of the deadliest natural disasters in recorded history. The direct results caused major disruptions in living conditions in Indonesia, Sri Lanka, India and Thailand. And finally, on 1 October 2005, a second series of bomb attacks occurred in Bali. Bombs exploded at two sites in the Jimbaran Beach Resort and in Kuta. The terrorist attack claimed the lives of 20 people and injured more than 100 others, once again reminding international tourists of the 'risk perception' related to travel to Bali and Indonesia.

Garuda also had its own 'internal' problem when on 7 September 2004, one of its passengers was murdered during a flight from Indonesia to Amsterdam via Singapore. Munir Said Thalib was a human rights activist who had earlier exposed human rights abuses by the secret service. He was travelling on Garuda flight 974 and was assassinated by off-duty pilot Pollycarpus Priyanto, who slipped arsenic into his drink some time before the departure of the flight's second leg to Amsterdam. The passenger felt unwell several hours after departure from Singapore, during which time he was checked by a doctor who happened to be on board. The man was moved to the business-class cabin to sleep. He died approximately two hours prior to arrival in Amsterdam. The murder sparked an international controversy, during which time Priyanto, along with CEO Indra Setiawan and deputy Rohainil Aini were all convicted of his murder, although it had been alleged it was under orders from the Indonesian State Intelligence Agency, Badan Intelijen Negara. The airline was found negligent in failing to perform an emergency landing and was ordered to pay compensation to Munir's widow, but failed to do so. Former State Intelligence Agency deputy chairman Muchdi Purwoprandjono was acquitted of all charges due to a lack of evidence. An article in the *Jakarta Post* on 19 September 2011 reported the filing of a case review to challenge the acquittal of the deputy chairman 'would be against the law', according to the attorney general.

All these facts, in such a short period of time, had seriously affected Garuda, which deferred an earlier order for six Boeing 777s and another order for 18 Boeing 737-800s planned to replace the ageing Boeing 737 classic fleet. However, by 2005, the airline had recovered from its economic problems and swapped its order for six Boeing 777s for ten Boeing 787-8 Dreamliners. However, the operational problems would remain.

Soon, other problems would arise. On 7 March 2007, Garuda flight 200, originating in Jakarta and headed for Yogjakarta, crashed on approach to the Adisucipto International Airport in Yogjakarta. Twenty passengers and one crew member were killed. Luckily, 112 passengers survived the crash. Despite a faulty approach, with excessive speed and a steep descent, and the resulting warnings of the co-pilot and flight systems, the pilot attempted to land his Boeing 737-400. The aircraft touched down 2,820ft beyond the runway threshold at a speed of 221 knots. The aircraft overran the end of the runway, went through the perimeter fence, was heavily damaged when it crossed a road and stopped in a nearby rice field. A fuel-fed fire raged that could not be reached by airport fire suppression vehicles. An international investigation concluded that the pilot failed to react to different warnings, as he was focused on trying to make the first approach work. As of March 2007, Garuda had implemented a new fuel efficiency incentive that awarded a salary bonus if fuel consumption for a flight was lower than nominal, but the captain denied that this had influenced his decision not to abort the landing. Subsequently, captain Komas was arrested and charged with several counts of manslaughter, but his conviction was overturned by the High Court's finding that the prosecutors had failed to prove that the pilot was convincingly guilty of a crime.

At that time, Garuda Indonesia had one of the worst safety records among the world's national carriers. In an article in the *Daily Telegraph*, published on 7 March 2007, Ashton Heath quotes Peter Harbison, the managing director of the Centre for Asia Pacific Aviation, as stating that the major accidents in Indonesian aviation were all caused by a combination of airports' and fleets' low safety standards and the poor weather conditions in the area, including severe thunderstorms and other forms of inclement weather. Notwithstanding the fact that Garuda had received the IATA operational safety audit certification from IATA, which means that it had completely met international aviation safety standards, the EU banned Garuda Indonesia, together with all other Indonesian airlines from flying into any European country. After sending a team of experts to Indonesia, led by the European Commission's air safety administrator, Federico Grandini, the EU stated that the safety reforms implemented after the Garuda crash were a step in the right direction for the EU to consider lifting the ban but still did not satisfy the EU's aviation safety standards, and thus it did not lift its ban. This decision thwarted Garuda's plans to resume services to Europe after it suspended flights to Amsterdam and Rome in 2005, following the decrease in international air traffic in the preceding years. Finally, the European ban was lifted in July 2009, after which Garuda began evaluating services to Amsterdam and other European destinations. In the meantime, Garuda calculated the ban had cost $1.5m a month in lost sales.

Fortunately, Garuda's management used the period of the ban to consider a new strategy for the future. In July 2009, the carrier announced an aggressive five-year expansion plan known as the Quantum Leap. The plan involved an image overhaul, including changing the airline's livery, staff uniform and logo. But besides these cosmetic changes, the airline also planned on nearly doubling the size of its fleet from 62 to 116 aircraft. The Quantum Leap also planned to boost annual passenger numbers to 27.6 million by 2014, up from 10.4 million at the time of the programme launch. This figure was to be reached through increasing domestic and international destinations from 41 to 62. According to Emirsyah Satar (the new CEO of Garuda), the fleet expansion would be supported by the ordering of sophisticated aircraft like the Airbus A330, Boeing 737-800 NG and Boeing 777ER.

On 23 July 2009, Indonesia's president, Susilo Bambang Yudhoyono, presided over the presentation of Garuda's 'new look'. The carrier showed off its new glass-oriented headquarters and two aircraft, an Airbus A330-200 and Boeing 737-800NG, representing several more that wouldn't be arriving until 2014. At the same time, it was announced Garuda planned to restart services to Amsterdam with a stopover in Dubai, using an Airbus A330-200. Garuda's cabin service had been refreshed as the 'Garuda Indonesia Experience'. It encapsulated all that represent Indonesia, from the design and colours of the livery (palm trees and bamboo rivers) to the music and cuisine associated with the country's various regions. 'Coming into our cabin will be like being welcomed into an Indonesian home', said the CEO. All these steps were deemed necessary to make the airline profitable again, and among other things, to find an answer to the growth of other Indonesian airlines, especially Lion Air, which had overtaken Garuda in terms of the number of aircraft in its fleet. Lion Air had been established in October 1999 and started up services on 30 June 2000. On 26 May 2005, the airline had signed an order for the purchase of 60 modern Boeing 737-900ERs. Lion Air's competition was even more important as Garuda had to suspend its Citilink operations in 2008. It relaunched the brand in January 2009 after replacing the remaining Fokker F28s with two Boeing 737-300s and a single Boeing 737-400. During Citilink's suspension, Lion Air had managed to book many Citilink passengers on its own flights.

In 1997, Garuda received the first of five Boeing 737-500s. (Jozef Mols collection)

Boeing 737-800s became the backbone of Garuda's fleet. (Erlando Day)

Because of the deregulation of air traffic, the Lion Air Group could set up full-fare subsidiary, Batik Air. (Gyrostat (Wikimedia, CC-BY-SA 4.0))

Because of the deregulation, several 'bare bone' airlines could start up. (Jozef Mols)

Garuda transferred its older Fokker F28s to its subsidiary, Citilink. (Jozef Mols)

Garuda also received its first Boeing 737-800NG. (Vismay Bhadra)

Chapter 6
Into the New Millennium

One can say the new millennium, with new hopes and prospects for Garuda, started in 2007 after the lifting of the EU embargo. Along with initiatives in business development in 2005, a new management team took office and formulated new plans for the future of the company. In 2009, Garuda strengthened its fleet with the arrival of Airbus A330-300 and Boeing 737-800 aircraft. Both types were equipped with in-flight entertainment and audio and video-on-demand in every seat. On 2 June 2010, the first Garuda flight (an Airbus A330-200) landed at Amsterdam Schiphol Airport after the lifting of the European embargo.

In 2008, Garuda had announced that its subsidiary, GMF AeroAsia, would be listed on the Indonesian Stock Exchange in 2008. However, due to the financial crisis in 2008, the stock offering was delayed until 2009. The successful completion of the company's debt restructuring programme, however, opened the way for Garuda to go public on 11 February 2011. The company officially became a public company after a public offering of 6,335,738,000 shares, listed on the Indonesia Stock Exchange with the Indonesian government retaining a majority of the shares. The initial public offering (IPO) could not count on the hoped-for success, as the shares offered were overpriced compared to shares of other airlines in the region, especially with revenues under pressure prior to the offering due to soaring global oil prices. Therefore, 47 per cent of the shares offered remained unsold, leading to them being absorbed by the underwriters of the IPO. PT Trans Asia bought a 10.9 per cent stake of the unsold IPO shares from the underwriters on 27 April 2012. This company is owned by Chairul Tanjung, one of Indonesia's richest businessmen, who paid US $166.8m for this stake. The original shares opened on the stock exchange at 750 rupiah per share, but the price fell as much as 23 per cent immediately after the introduction on the stock exchange.

An earlier cancelled order for Boeing 787 aircraft was exchanged for an order for ten Boeing 777-300ERs instead, which Garuda would take delivery of in 2013 to be used on long-haul flights to Europe and medium-haul flights within Asia. The new Boeings would also be used on the busy Jakarta–Denpasar route.

In May 2011, Garuda announced plans for a spin-off of Citilink. The airline, which had been established as Garuda's low-cost subsidiary in 2001, became a separate business entity in the first quarter of 2012, with a full brand overhaul, including a new livery design, new website, new cabin interior design and cabin crew uniforms, plus new advertising and marketing strategies. But above all, an integral part of this plan was for Citilink to secure 25 new Airbus A320s and to use these new and more economical aircraft to expand into a significant regional low-cost carrier. On 9 August 2011, Garuda finalised an order for 25 Airbus A320 aircraft with options for 25 more. By the end of the year, Garuda was seeking even more second-hand A320s in preparation for the launch of the proposed international Citilink services. And in December 2012, Citilink placed an order for 24 ATR 72-600s with options for 25 more. A direct order for 25 additional A320neos followed in January 2013. The expectation was that by 2015, Citilink would contribute 30 per cent of Garuda's revenue. By the end of 2013, Citilink had carried eight million passengers and was running at a load factor of 85 per cent with an 'on-time arrival' of 87 per cent. By May 2015, the fleet consisted of four Boeing 737-300s, four Boeing 737-500s and 34 Airbus A320s. However, since its transition from a unit to a subsidiary of Garuda in 2012, Citilink was consistently unprofitable.

In 2011, Garuda started targeting online sales in an effort to boost the airline's revenue in co-operation with Visa, Mastercard and Paypal. Furthermore, in co-operation with Bank Mandiri, BCA and BII, the airline also developed a system for online debit card payments.

Looking for international expansion, Garuda started flights to the Middle East and Europe in a codeshare agreement with Etihad Airways in 2012. As a result, the Jakarta–Dubai–Amsterdam route was changed into a Jakarta–Abu Dhabi–Amsterdam route. Also in 2012, the airline formed a partnership with Liverpool FC through a sponsorship deal. This way, Garuda became the 'Official Partner of Liverpool Football Club' and 'Official Global Airline Partner of Liverpool Football Club'. Liverpool, for its part, would broadcast a series of six-minute advertisement videos during matches at the Reds' home ground for the 2012–13 season. The agreement was expected to assist Garuda in expanding its international market, as well as trim the airline's advertising costs.

In order to further facilitate international travel, Garuda started offering immigration services on board its flights. This meant tourists didn't have to queue up to get a visa at the airport any more. Under the 'Immigration on Board' service, started up in 2013 (but stopped in 2014), passengers received their visa from immigration officials during the flight, prior to arrival. The service was available to all passengers, regardless of their ticket class. The same year, Garuda launched its 'in-flight connectivity' facility on Airbus A330 aircraft for both executive and economy class, allowing passengers to connect to an internet connection via Wi-Fi during the flight. The same service had already been offered previously on Boeing 777-300 aircraft. The service was intended to provide added value for passengers because they could continue their business activities during the flight.

Starting in the fourth quarter of 2013, the airline planned to operate a direct Jakarta–London Gatwick route. The flight was to be operated six times a week by Boeing 777-300ER aircraft in the light of increased business transactions between Indonesia and the United Kingdom. By the end of the year, Garuda, however, postponed the start-up of the direct flight and had to refund or re-accommodate passengers who had booked tickets on the flight in the first months of heavily promoted sales. At the time of the planned launch of the non-stop route to London, the Jakarta airport was not ready to service fully loaded 777s, as the airport was only certified to handle weights of up to 120 tons. An upgrade to 132 tons was needed for Garuda to operate the 777 at full capacity on the route to London. This forced Garuda to underuse its brand-new 777 flagship fleet on long-haul flights. A planned Jakarta–Paris launch was also impacted by this situation. As a result, Garuda had to revise its long-haul strategy, as the situation created overcapacity. Furthermore, as a result of unfavourable market conditions, Garuda had to respond by deferring plans to launch new services to India and the Philippines. Besides, since the introduction of the 777s, Garuda's international load factors had plummeted to below 70 per cent.

In December 2013, Garuda also announced a comprehensive partnership pact with ANA, Japan's leading airline group. Under this agreement, the two airlines would codeshare on flights between the two countries and would allow passengers to be able to collect and redeem miles on the frequent-flyer programme of both airlines. As of 30 March 2014, ANA would operate a new route between Tokyo Haneda Airport and Jakarta Airport, followed by Garuda a few days later on the same route. In 2013, Garuda also announced a codeshare arrangement with Indian carrier Jet Airways, providing seamless connectivity to various destinations on the combined networks of the two airlines. A codeshare agreement with Korean Air allowed Garuda to add two weekly frequencies on the Jakarta–Seoul route. Plans for further expansion in the European market were shelved.

In 2014, it was decided to adjust the Boeing 777-300ER route plans to focus on Japan, rather than on the United Kingdom and Australia. This U-turn in Garuda's wide-body fleet deployment strategy reflected the intense competition in the Southeast Asia–Europe and Australia–Europe markets,

A Garuda Indonesia Boeing 777-300ER. (Garuda Indonesia)

Another Boeing 777-300ER in flight. (Björn Van Brussel)

A Boeing 777-300ER at Jakarta Airport. (Jozef Mols collection)

The economy cabin of an Airbus A330. (Rinaldo Wibyanto)

compared with more attractive expansion possibilities within Asia. Therefore, the planned non-stop Jakarta–London Gatwick and Jakarta–Amsterdam flights would be dropped in favour of a Jakarta–Amsterdam–London service. Another reason for this decision was the fact that the London–Jakarta direct market was not large enough to support the operation of a Boeing 777-300. Finding enough connecting passengers to make the route viable would have been difficult. Indeed, at the London end, Garuda had been unable to secure slots at London Heathrow Airport. Before, the airline had planned to launch a daily Jakarta–Sydney service with Boeing 777-300ER equipment, replacing the Airbus A330 used earlier. This would have resulted in a 'same plane – one stop' service from London via Jakarta to Sydney.

On the domestic market, Garuda made efforts to further expand its market share. With the introduction of ATR 72-600 aircraft, the airline was able to connect Bali to areas with runways below 5,200ft. Under the 'Explore Flight, Explore Indonesia' sub-brand, Garuda opened routes from Denpasar to Labuan Bajo (Komodo Island) and Ende (Flores) and between Denpasar and Bima (Sumbawa island) and Mataram (Lombok). It was also hoped that the introduction of such flights would open up exotic destinations to international tourists. The first flight on this route left Denpasar in December 2013. At that time, Garuda had received two ATR aircraft. Until 2017, as many as 35 aircraft of the type were planned to be delivered to strengthen Garuda's short-haul fleet, which also included some Bombardier CRJ1000 aircraft.

In 2014, Garuda acquired an additional 21.25 per cent stake in Gapura Angkasa, becoming the majority owner of this company, which offers ground-handling services, warehousing, executive lounge management and hospitality services in airports across the nation. Gapura was set up in 1998 as a joint venture between Garuda and Angkasa Pura I, a state-owned airport operator. Also in 2014, the Jakarta Halim Perdanakusuma Airport reopened for scheduled commercial passenger jet flights, slightly relieving congestion at Jakarta Soekarno-Hatta Airport. On 10 January 2014, Garuda's budget subsidiary, Citilink, became the first of at least four major Indonesian carriers to launch flights from Halim with eight frequencies on four domestic routes. But Garuda, Indonesia Air Asia and Lion Air also soon followed. Initially, Lion Air had planned to move the new full-service subsidiary, Batik Air, from Soekarno-Hatta to Halim, but in a change of strategy, it decided to move selected Lion Air operated frequencies on major trunk routes. Batik Air continued to operate from Soekarno-Hatta, in order to compete with Garuda's full-service flights, whereas Lion Air's budget flights moved to Halim to compete with Garuda's Citilink budget operation. Of course, moving to Halim Airport is only a limited solution for Soekarno-Hatta's congestion problems. Halim has only one runway and no parallel taxiway; the terminal building is old and the apron is small. Furthermore, as Halim is also used by the Air Force, there is a risk of commercial flights being delayed when there are military training flights. By the end of 2014, some of Garuda's smaller competitors on the domestic market had gone out of business. Merpati – once a Garuda subsidiary – went bankrupt, whereas Sky Aviation and Tigerair Mandala also suspended operations. This resulted in a more rational level of capacity in the domestic market. Therefore, Garuda decided to focus on further strengthening its domestic operations while decreasing its focus on international expansion and relying more on SkyTeam to grow its global footprint.

On 5 March 2014, Garuda became the fifth flag carrier in the fast-growing Southeast Asian region to join a global alliance. With Garuda as a new member, SkyTeam surpassed Star Alliance as the largest alliance in Southeast Asia by seat capacity, with about a 16 per cent share compared to 14 per cent for Star and 10 per cent for the Oneworld alliance. Entering the SkyTeam alliance was a major step for Garuda, which planned to introduce new non-stop services to Amsterdam and London. When a new Boeing 777-300ER was delivered to Garuda on 28 October 2015, it was painted in a special SkyTeam livery. (The first aircraft of this type had been delivered already, starting in 2013.) At the same time, Garuda made it clear it would try to intensify its co-operation with Chinese members of SkyTeam, including China Eastern, China Southern and Xiamen airlines, as the China–Indonesia market was growing rapidly. At that time, Garuda was the largest flag carrier in Southeast Asia in terms of total seat capacity and fleet size, but it was still a relatively small international player. In 2014, Garuda allocated 79 per cent of its seat capacity to the domestic market, according to CAPA (Centre for Aviation) and OAG (Official Aviation Guide) data. The domestic market accounted for about 50 per cent of Garuda's revenue. In 2013, Garuda had only carried 3.8m international passengers, compared with 15.8m domestic passengers. (Citilink, which was not part of the SkyTeam alliance, carried 5.3m domestic passengers.)

In late 2014, Garuda became one of seven airlines to earn the prestigious five-star rating from Skytrax, marking the end of the five-year 'Quantum Leap' programme. Earlier, in 2013, the airline had already won the Skytrax World's Best Cabin Crew award. CEO Emirsyah Sater considered his mission to be completed and he resigned, appointing former Citilink chief, Arif Wibowo, as his successor. Following his appointment, Wibowo embarked on a 'quick wins' cost-cutting drive to cut down on losses while boosting revenue through various measures, including cancelling unprofitable routes and increasing staff efficiency. At the same time, he announced his plan to buy 90 new aircraft from both Boeing and Airbus during the 2015 Paris Air Show. These orders included 80 narrow bodies for domestic and regional operations, including 30 Boeing 737-MAX, 20 Boeing Dreamliners and 30 Airbus A350 XWB aircraft. Garuda also signed a letter of intent for 14 Airbus A330-900neo aircraft (including seven cancellations from an existing Airbus A330-300 order). At the same time, the airline wanted to defer aircraft deliveries for its intercontinental operations while accelerating aircraft retirement. Both moves were aimed at reducing capacity (or slowing capacity growth) in response to challenging conditions in the international market. The airline had already received five Boeing 777s and still had five more on order. Some of these aircraft were used on Saudi Arabia flights, supplemented by two Boeing 747s to cater for the seasonally higher demand for these flights. In fact, Garuda did not need more Boeing 777s, or certainly not all ten aircraft. Its fleet of Airbus A330s was better suited for routes within Asia Pacific.

A Garuda Airbus A330-300 arriving at Denpasar Airport. (Jozef Mols)

The cabin of a Boeing 737-800. (Frederick Lee)

Not only the fleet but also the uniforms of the cabin crew were renewed. (Master Films/H Goussé/Airbus for Garuda Indonesia)

The Garuda Group fleet at the end of June 2014

Aircraft type	Total	Operational lease	Owned/financial lease
Boeing 737-300	1		1
Boeing 737-500	4		4
Boeing 737-800NG	70	70	
Bombardier CRJ1000	15	9	6
ATR 72-600	5	5	
Total narrow body	95	84	11
Boeing 747-400	2		2
Boeing 777ER	5	5	
Airbus A330-200	11	11	
Airbus A330-300	7	1	6
Total wide body	25	17	8
Citilink fleet			
Boeing 737-300	4		4
Airbus A320-200	25	25	
Total Citilink fleet	29	25	4

Source: Garuda Indonesia results presentation for the first half of 2014

Garuda ordered a series of ATR 72-600 aircraft to serve airports with a short runway, and the new aircraft became very popular with passengers on 'thin' routes. (Bantair Airlines)

With the ATR 72-600, Garuda was able to compete with other airlines that used small aircraft for flights to destinations with short runways. (Ariodilah Virgantara)

Garuda also added some Bombardier CRJ1000 jets to its fleet to be used on 'thin' routes. (Pauli Hankonen)

Although the Bombardier CRJ1000 jet seemed to be the right aircraft for Garuda's needs, later on the company was looking to sell them again as they did not meet expectations. (Ariodilah Virgantara)

A Garuda Citilink Boeing 737 400. (Jozef Mols collection)

Citilink placed a large order for Airbus A320s to be used on domestic routes. (Adhe Bhisma Chendikia)

Garuda transferred ATR 72-600s to its subsidiary, Citilink. (Jozef Mols collection)

Citilink also performs cargo flights. (Ariodilah Virgantara)

Chapter 7

Garuda Today

Whereas Garuda was still considering opening routes to Paris and Frankfurt, it was announced the airline would start up a service between Jakarta and Mumbai with a stop in Bangkok by the end of 2016. As the American Federal Aviation Authority lifted the ban on Garuda in August 2016, the airline also considered opening routes to the United States by 2017. On 19 April 2016, Flight Global indicated that Garuda had placed an order for 14 Airbus A330neo twinjets, replacing an order for seven Airbus A330-300s that was cancelled earlier. The first deliveries were due to take place in 2019. The new aircraft are powered by Rolls-Royce Trent 7,000 engines. These decisions were made notwithstanding weak financial results in the first half of 2016. Garuda's international load factor was only 70 per cent through the first eight months of 2016, as the airline struggled to fill additional seats generated by an 18 per cent increase in capacity. The long-haul routes had particularly struggled, driving the books into the red. It was not the first time international expansion had a negative impact on profitability. Recent international expansion focused on Europe, China and Saudi Arabia. Garuda had launched a route from Jakarta via Singapore to London Heathrow in 2016 alongside six flights a week to Amsterdam. All these flights operated with a stop in Singapore on the outbound sector, but operated non-stop on the return leg of the flight. The six rotations per week on the Jakarta–London route were reduced to five by late 2016. All flights were operated using Boeing 777-300ER equipment.

In Saudi Arabia, Garuda increased its presence by introducing routes to Jeddah from secondary Indonesian cities and a new seasonal service from Jakarta to Medina. In the Southeast Asian region, Garuda had only slightly increased capacity with its additional flights to Singapore. Presence in Australia had already been slightly reduced in 2015. Taiwan was dropped completely, whereas capacity to Japan had been dropped in 2014. On the other hand, the carrier had increased its visibility in Hong Kong and China by launching flights between Denpasar (Bali) to Beijing and Shanghai. A Bali–Guangzhou service was launched in late 2015 using Boeing 737-800 aircraft (upgraded to the Airbus A330-300). All other flights to China were operated by Airbus A330-300s prior to being upgraded to Boeing 777-300ER aircraft by the end of 2016. The routes to and from Bali and China, however, had become very competitive, as several foreign carriers, including China Eastern, China Southern and Xiamen Airlines, had also added capacity to the route, and Chinese low-cost carrier Lucky Air launched services to Bali as well. And on the domestic side, Lion Air had also responded to the increased growth of tourism in Bali by adding services to China.

But besides these changes, Garuda had to further adjust its international network, reducing capacity across its medium- and long-haul networks. Capacity to Australia and Japan, two of Garuda's largest international markets, was cut as part of a restructuring of its unprofitable international operations. These cuts were a response to overcapacity and intensifying competition, but left an opening for competitors like low-cost start-up Indonesia Air Asia X. The restructuring included the suspension of services to Brisbane and the shelving of aircraft to launch Nagoya and the reduction in frequency to Tokyo. As for the route between Jakarta and London, Garuda had to make difficult decisions. It was rumoured at some time that Garuda might cut its London service entirely. Garuda planned to rely on connections with partner KLM to serve the Amsterdam–London part of a flight that would connect Jakarta with Amsterdam. This could have been a wise decision given KLM's strong UK network and the relatively high cost for operating the Amsterdam–London leg on Garuda flights. But pulling out of London would have been a bitter pill to swallow. Garuda had invested heavily in the UK market, setting up an office in London and building its brand through sponsoring Liverpool Football Club. Garuda's image had already suffered by twice postponing the London launch and dropping the initial plan for non-stop services. On the other hand, Garuda had been hoping to start up a Jakarta–London–New York route if the American FAA would upgrade the airline to Category 1.

At the same time, Garuda was adjusting its fleet plan by negotiating early returns for several leased aircraft and pursuing subleases. The airline also planned to halt all aircraft deliveries for two to three years as part of an initiative to improve its financial position. Nevertheless, the airline still hoped to grow capacity by 10–12 per cent per year by improving utilisation of its existing fleet, which would result in lower unit costs and higher efficiencies. Therefore, Garuda started negotiations with manufacturers to defer Airbus A320neos, Airbus A330-900neos, Boeing 737 Max 8s and ATR 72-600s. At that time, the airline had 103 aircraft on order, including 50 Boeing 737 MAX 8s (ordered in 2014), 30 Airbus A320neos, 14 Airbus A330-900neos and nine ATR 72-600s. At the same time, Garuda also set an objective of not taking delivery of new aircraft in 2018 and 2019. It was, however, uncertain if this plan could work, as all buyer-furnished equipment for the A320neos had already been acquired. And halting the delivery of Boeing 737-800 MAX aircraft also seemed unlikely after Garuda took delivery of its first of the type in December 2017. While renegotiating the contract with Boeing was difficult, the Indonesian website Bisnis.com revealed on 26 January 2019, that Garuda had cancelled all outstanding orders for this type of aircraft following the crashes involving two Boeing 737 MAX 8 aircraft. However, Garuda agreed to exchange the order for 34 Boeing 737 MAX 10 aircraft, the first to be delivered in 2020. And in 2017, Garuda operated its last Boeing 747 service after the last aircraft touched down in Makassar from Medina on a return flight for the Hajj pilgrimage. It was then ferried to Jakarta the following day for retirement.

These intentions should be seen in light of Garuda's worsening financial position. In the first three quarters of 2017, the group had incurred an operating loss of $109m compared with an operating profit of $4m the year before. In the same light, the Boeing 737-800 fleet was reconfigured to boost the number of seats, which would improve efficiency and result in an increase in capacity on some short-haul international routes.

In the domestic market, business was booming for Garuda's Citilink operations. The carrier intended to expand its operations from the Jakarta Halim Perdanakusuma Airport and form a new hub in Medan (Sumatra). In 2015, the airline accounted for approximately 12 per cent of the Indonesian domestic market, up from only 3 per cent in 2011. Passenger traffic grew by 24 per cent in 2015, while its full-service parent company Garuda grew by 10 per cent in the same period. In 2015, Garuda transported 19.4m passengers on domestic routes, capturing an estimated 24 per cent of Indonesia's domestic market that year. Citilink operated a fleet of 36 all-economy Airbus A320s with 180 seats, with bases in Bali, Batam, Jakarta Soekarno-Hatta, Jakarta Halim and Surabaya (and later also Medan). Operations were limited to domestic routes with the exception of some charter flights. The Garuda group had benefited from the consolidation in the Indonesian market with the suspension of Batavia in 2013 and Merpati (once a Garuda subsidiary, sold to the government later), Sky Aviation and Tigerair Mandala in 2014. The four airlines had accounted for nearly 20 per cent of the Indonesian domestic market. At the same time, the group had been winning back market share from Lion Air, which had grown at a phenomenal pace in the previous decade to become Indonesia's largest domestic carrier in 2009. In 2015, however, Lion Air's market share had experienced its first drop in 2015 after some scandals involving cabin crew using drugs prior to their flight. But its full-service subsidiary, Batikair, and low-cost subsidiary, Wings Air, still showed growth. The results of the Garuda Group were

A Garuda Boeing 737 in its special 72nd birthday livery. (Garuda Indonesia)

Competitor Lion Air also adjusted its capacity, in response to the increased demand, by obtaining Airbus A330 equipment for both its Indonesian and Thai fleets. (dn280)

impressive if one takes into account that the overall Indonesian market for domestic transportation experienced a very slow growth in the period between 2010 and 2015, owing to a weaker economy and the rapid depreciation of the Indonesian rupiah, which had an impact on consumer spending. To compensate for these economic factors, the Indonesian government had reduced the price floor by 10 per cent, enabling airlines to stimulate demand and persuade budget-conscious passengers to take more trips. It should be noted that the Indonesian government still regulated the aviation sector, which was vital for the connectivity between the many islands of the archipelago. However, Lion Air was the largest beneficiary of the lower-price floor, as its average fares had historically been lower than Citilink's. Indeed, Lion Air had a lower cost structure. As Lion Air was able to further reduce its ticket prices, Citilink had to follow. Lower fares stimulated market demand in numbers of passengers, but put pressure on profit margins. On the other hand, however, Citilink was able to be profitable during off-peak periods, operating several international charter flights, mainly to mainland China. Most of these flights originated in Bali where Citilink had based four A320s. Other flights departed in Manado, a world famous diving site. In early 2015, Citilink had also launched five weekly charter flights to Jeddah with fuel stops in Medan and Mumbai. A previous international flight, started in 2014 between Surabaya and Johor Bahru in southern Malaysia, had been stopped after only one month. International flights did not force Citilink to reduce domestic capacity, as new aircraft were delivered to the fleet in 2015. The charters were attractive to Citilink, as all the seats were completely underwritten by travel agents, guaranteeing a profit on every flight. Therefore, the international charter market was logical, as launching regular international flights would have represented a significant and risky investment. Since its transition from a Garuda unit to a Garuda subsidiary in 2012, Citilink's bookkeeping had always been in the red until the third quarter of 2014 when the airline made a modest profit of $4m. Profitability is important as it would make it easier for Citilink to pursue a potential spin-off and IPO of shares on the stock market. A possible IPO for Citilink had already been suggested by Garuda earlier. But whereas it was sensible for Citilink to focus on the domestic market and profitability, this was not necessarily the best strategy for Garuda given the huge challenges the group was facing in the international market. But in 2014, Citilink had rejected offers from Garuda to take over some of the international routes. Garuda considered that Citilink, as a low-cost carrier, would be a more suitable option for leisure-focused routes that, at the time, were unprofitable at the full-service brand.

In the meantime, Garuda had received several important awards. In 2017, the airline achieved Skytrax's five-star airline rating as well as winning the prestigious 'World's Best Cabin Crew' for four consecutive years (2014–17). Earlier, the airline had already obtained the 'Best Economy Class' award in 2013 and the 'World's Most Loved Airline' in 2016. But also, subsidiary Citilink received an important award: in 2017, it received the '4-Star Low-Cost Airline' award from Skytrax. In 2017, Wibowo retired as CEO to be replaced by Pahala Nugraha Mansury, and later the same year by I Gusti Ngurah Askara Danadiputra, better known as Ari Askhara. During Askhara's term in office, live acoustic concerts were introduced on domestic flights, leading to great criticism. He also decided to reopen a Denpasar–London route with a transit stop in Medan.

On 6 September 2018, the *Nikkei Asia Review* revealed that Garuda would open a new route to New York and increase its flights to Los Angeles through a new codesharing agreement with Japan Airlines. Earlier, the Indonesian airline had sought to fly to American destinations on its own, but the inability to obtain landing slots at a Japanese airport for a stopover en route and subsequent financial constraints thwarted its plans. Garuda already had a codeshare deal with Delta Airlines on a route to Los Angeles via Haneda Airport, and with China Airlines to San Francisco via the Taiwan Taoyuan International Airport near Taipei. The new codesharing agreement would expand Garuda's American business when the airline would start a service to New York and Los Angeles via Narita.

At the same time, the deal included shared flights between Indonesian and Japanese cities, including Jakarta, Denpasar, Surabaya and Yogjakarta in Indonesia and Tokyo, Fukuoka, Nagoya and Sapporo (Chitose) in Japan. On 27 November 2018, Garuda also resumed its London Heathrow to Jakarta service on a three-times-a-week non-stop service, operated by a Boeing 777-300. Nevertheless, Garuda also experienced some legal problems when publishing its 2018 balance sheet. In April 2019, two independent commissioners of the airline said the 2018 Annual Report was not in accordance with the Statement of Financial Accounting Standards, and thus decided not to sign the report. Both the Ministry of Finance and the Financial Services Authority found various violations within the report. The airline and its auditors were issued with a penalty. A revised 2018 financial report showed that Garuda suffered a net loss of $175.2m in 2018, instead of the net profit of $5.1m reported in the controversial balance sheet. In the new balance sheet, Garuda also reported a total revenue of $4.37bn, the same as in the rejected report. However, in the new financial statement the airline's other income totalled only $38.8m, a far cry from the $278.8m recorded in the previous financial report.

The same year, the Transportation Minister, Budi Karya Sumadi, welcomed Merpati's plan to resume its operations on condition the airline met the conditions that the state requires concerning aircraft and employee procurement. Once a Garuda subsidiary, Merpati would resume operations under the direct supervision of the government. And still in the same year, Garuda, through its subsidiary Citilink, took over operations as well as financial management of Sriwijaya Air. This was realised in the form of joint operations carried out by Citilink with Sriwijaya and PT NAM Air.

Lion Air's subsidiary, Wings Air, was an important competitor, as it was not hurt by scandals surrounding its parent company. (Jozef Mols)

Garuda started a joint venture with Sriwijaya Air. (Jozef Mols)

Garuda participated in the management company of several Indonesian airports like Denpasar International Airport. (Bali Denpasar International Airport)

Halim Perdanakusuma Airport, where Citilink has a hub, is also used by the military and the government. (Angkatan Udara)

Garuda participated in Gapura Angkasa, which also handles ground services. (Gapura Angkasa)

The departure of a Hajj pilgrimage flight from Halim Perdanakusuma Airport. (Gapura Angkasa)

Garuda's business class lounge – international. (Garuda Indonesia)

Above and below: Garuda's business class lounge – domestic. (Garuda Indonesia)

Above and below: Garuda's first class lounge. (Garuda Indonesia)

Chapter 8
Going Forward

On 5 December 2019, CEO Askhara was fired from his position for smuggling a classic Harley-Davidson motorcycle and Brompton folding bicycle, which were found by the Soekarno-Hatta International Airport's customs and excise team inside a recently delivered Airbus A330-900 aircraft. Earlier, the CEO had already been subject of criticism as he introduced live music on board some domestic flights, turning the cabin of the aircraft into a 'flying disco'. Askhara was replaced in his function by Irfan Setiaputra.

But this was only the tip of the iceberg. During the investigation that followed the smuggling case, it was revealed that Askhara and other directors of the airline made various policies that harmed Garuda flight attendants, such as dismissal without explanation, additional flight hours and discrimination between employees. Later, it was revealed that many flight attendants had experienced sexual harassment and were forced into prostitution by Askhara and these directors. Some flight attendants confirmed that the vice president in charge of cabin crew, Roni Eka Mirsa, was the pimp for the prostitution gang.

On 7 May, the airline resumed some services after being grounded for some time due to COVID-19. On 14 May 2020, as a result of the COVID-19 pandemic and its worldwide impact on aviation and airlines, Garuda furloughed 800 of its staff for at least three months. In June, the airline laid off 180 contracted pilots. At the same time, the airline offered early retirement packages for employees who were over 50 years old. The package was worth about 35 times the monthly wage, more than a usual retirement package, which was equal to 30 times the employee's monthly wage. The airline had indeed been forced to park 100 of its 142 aircraft as its daily flights had dropped by 70 per cent because of the government's large-scale social restrictions, but also because of a drop in consumer demand for air travel.

When the airline implemented face masks for the crew members in accordance with health regulations, to prevent the spread of the disease, passengers began to complain that they could not see the flight attendants' faces and were unable to tell their emotions because of the masks. In reaction, Garuda discontinued the use of face masks and stated it would look for alternative means of protection, such as face shields. Gloves for flights attendants would remain anyway. Whereas most airlines have by now introduced a range of COVID-19 protection measures aimed at protecting the health of passengers and crew, some – including Garuda – went even further. Garuda painted a mask onto its brand-new Airbus A330neo. It took 60 people and 120 hours for 'Neo' to wear a mask. Apart from launching this special livery, the airline is also holding a mask livery design competition with the theme 'Fly Your Design Through The Sky'. The carrier promised to paint the four best designs onto Garuda Indonesia aircraft. Although crews are no longer obliged to wear masks, passengers still are, like anywhere else in the world.

On the financial front, Garuda also had to solve serious problems. The airline managed to renegotiate the mature debt of $498.88m with its bondholders. The notes, known as 'Garuda Indonesia Global Sukuk Limited' would have matured on 3 June 2020. At that time, the state-owned airline had a total loan of $1.83bn with an equity position of only $720.62m. In light of the COVID-19 crisis, Garuda was of course seeking financial support from financial institutions and from the government.

Due to the COVID-19 pandemic, Garuda noticed an important expansion of e-commerce and hence an increase in demand for air cargo. It was therefore decided to enlarge the cargo fleet. The airline already operated a Boeing 737-300 and a Boeing 737-400, each with a carrying capacity of 15 to 18 tons. It was decided to add two more cargo aircraft; an Airbus A330 with a capacity of 60 tons and a Boeing 737-800 with a capacity of 23 tons. These two aircraft would be converted from passenger plane to cargo plane at the PT GMF Aero Asia Tbk subsidiary of Garuda. In the meantime, Garuda entered into a lease agreement with GECAS for two B737-800 Boeing-converted freighters to supplement three leased B737-300Fs from My Indo Airlines.

Optimising the number of flights and the fleet was, of course, another means of solving some problems. Therefore, the delivery of four Airbus A330-900neos was delayed. Not only did the airline delay deliveries, but it also deferred payment on 40 aircraft in the second quarter of 2020, which saved the airline about $100m in the short term. Garuda also renegotiated prices and terms, with 12 lessors, saving a further $30m annually. And it was rumoured the airline was seeking buyers for its Bombardier CRJ1000 fleet. The 18 aircraft were acquired, starting in 2012, to launch new air services starting up point-to-point services within Indonesia in an effort to bypass the country's congested hub in Jakarta. According to the airline, the aircraft were, however, ill-suited to its Southeast Asian operations. Garuda became dissatisfied with the type due to a lack of product support in the region. Furthermore, the type needs a runway of 6,500 feet, whereas the airline wanted an aircraft that could access short runways.

Amid the development in the global economy, following the outbreak of the COVID-19 crisis, the future seems uncertain for Garuda – but also for many other airlines worldwide. CEO Setiaputra stated that, in the next half year, the aviation industry would further deteriorate, as there is a lack of clarity about when the pandemic will end. Usually, Garuda's peak season is between May and June for travellers, which coincides with the end of Ramadan and school holidays. It was clear Garuda would not be able to operate Hajj flights in 2020. The company expected a 33 per cent decline in total revenue for the first quarter of 2020 due to falling passenger numbers and ticket prices.

In an effort to assist the Indonesian tourism industry and at the same time help Indonesian airlines to service the COVID-19 pandemic, Indonesian president Joko Widodo launched the idea to create a holding company, bringing together nine state-run companies including flag carrier Garuda and low-cost airline Citilink, plus companies that run major tourism sites. Companies in the tourism sector would include Hotel Indonesia Natour (which has 14 properties on Bali and elsewhere), the management of the Mandalika resort and the Labuan Bajo resort, as well as the Borobodur Temple and the department store Sarinah, selling Indonesian handicraft. Many observers believe the actual purpose of setting up the holding is to shake up Garuda's management. The airline indeed suffered a net loss of $723.26m in the first half of 2020, which is nearly as much as its total net capital. The government would provide $578.7m financial assistance into the holding company, but many object to a direct infusion of tax money because the government will only hold 60 per cent of the shares in the holding. If the holding was wholly state owned, there would be a clear public purpose in the efficiency drive and make state aid easier to justify. The set-up of the holding would turn out to be positive for Garuda, as it owes $76m to the airport management companies, which would also become part of the holding. Folding them all into a single holding company would make it much easier for Garuda to restructure its debts.

What the future will bring for Garuda is difficult to tell. The airline was already struggling with year-long financial problems. These are now aggravated by the worldwide COVID-19 crisis, which has hit all airlines. Nevertheless, CEO Irfan Setiaputra remains optimistic: 'We have to make tough decisions', he said in an interview with the *Jakarta Post* on 3 June 2020. 'Nevertheless, we believe that Garuda can improve its operational condition once more and survive these challenging times.' In 2019, well before the COVID-19 pandemic, 120 million people took a flight in Indonesia, a number that was estimated to double by the middle of the decade. But the events in 2020 have tempered these optimistic forecasts. It is clear the airline still has a long road ahead to get out of the crisis.

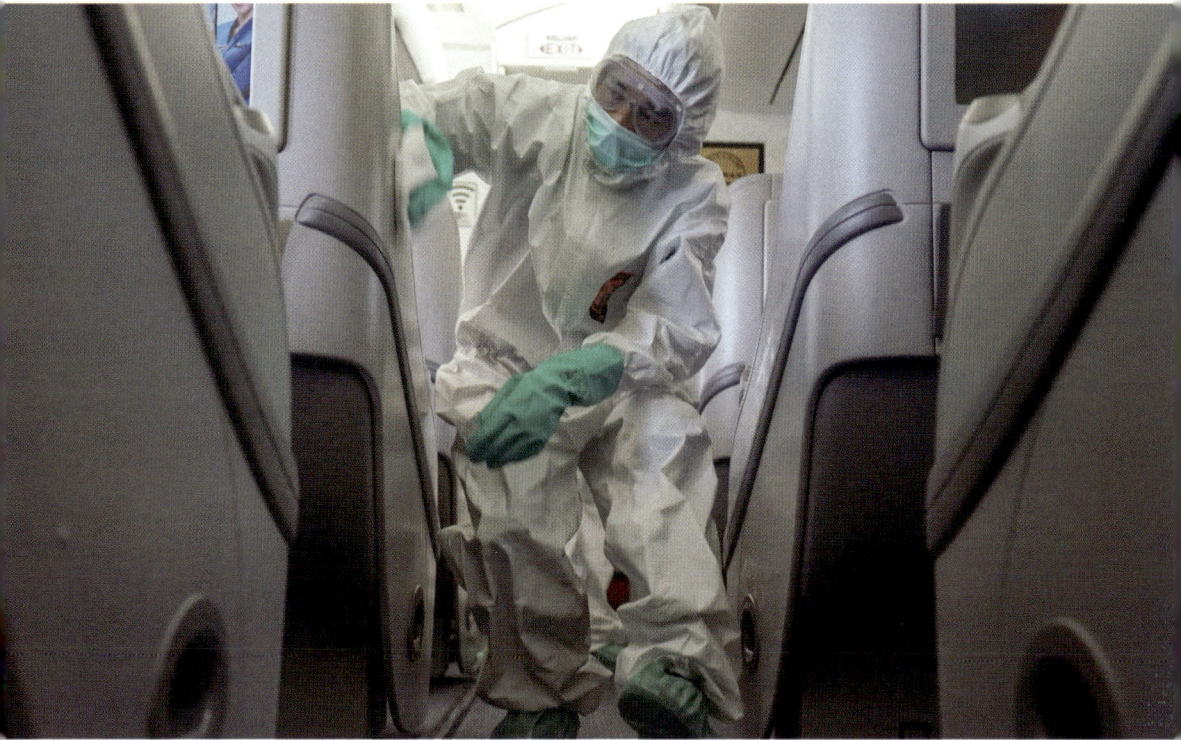

Disinfecting the cabin is one of the new tasks for Garuda staff. (Garuda Indonesia)

Garuda shows its 'face mask' nose art on several of its aircraft. (Garuda Indonesia)

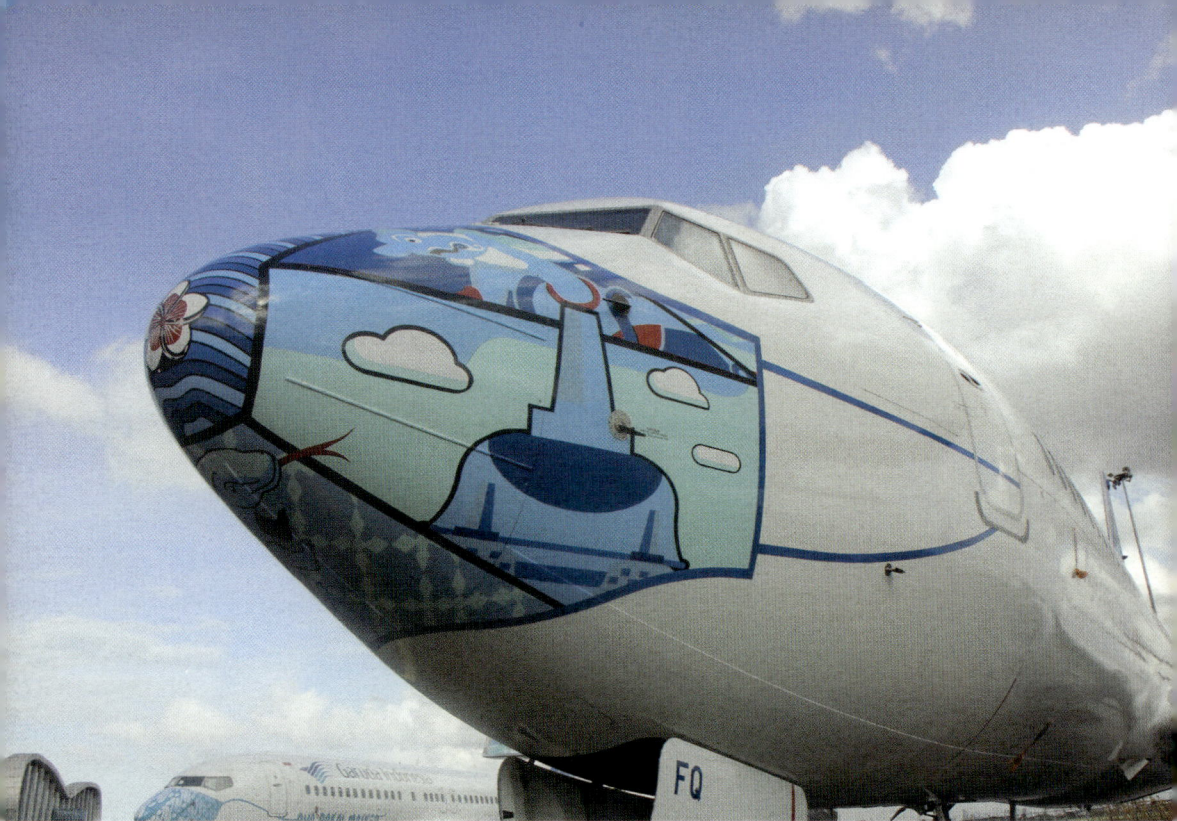

Above and below: This Garuda Indonesia Boeing 737-800 is wearing the 'Indonesian Pride' mask livery. (Garuda Indonesia)

A Boeing 777-300 shows of its 'corona mask' in China. (Weicheng Huang Zi)

The 'Membangan Masa Depan Bangsa'-mask livery is shown on this aircraft. (Garuda Indonesia)

An Airbus A330-900 with nose mask. (Akira Uekawa)

Left: The 'Sekar Jagat Nusantara' nose art reminds passengers to wear face masks. (Garuda Indonesia)

Below: This Boeing 737-800 is painted with the 'Terbang Tinggi dan Tetap Terlindungi' nose art. (Garuda Indonesia)

Above and below: Garuda Indonesia Safety Emergency Procedure (SEP) training. (Garuda Indonesia)

Warming up before Garuda Indonesia Safety Emergency (SEP) training. (Garuda Indonesia)

Garuda's operational centre in Jakarta. (Photo received from a former Garuda employee)

Garuda Indonesia cabin crew training. (Garuda Indonesia)

Whereas Garuda used face-mask nose art, subsidiary Citilink grabs attention with its colorful paint schemes. (Rachmat Dwi Putra)

Citilink aircraft are eye-catchers thanks to their publicity banners. (Chaity)

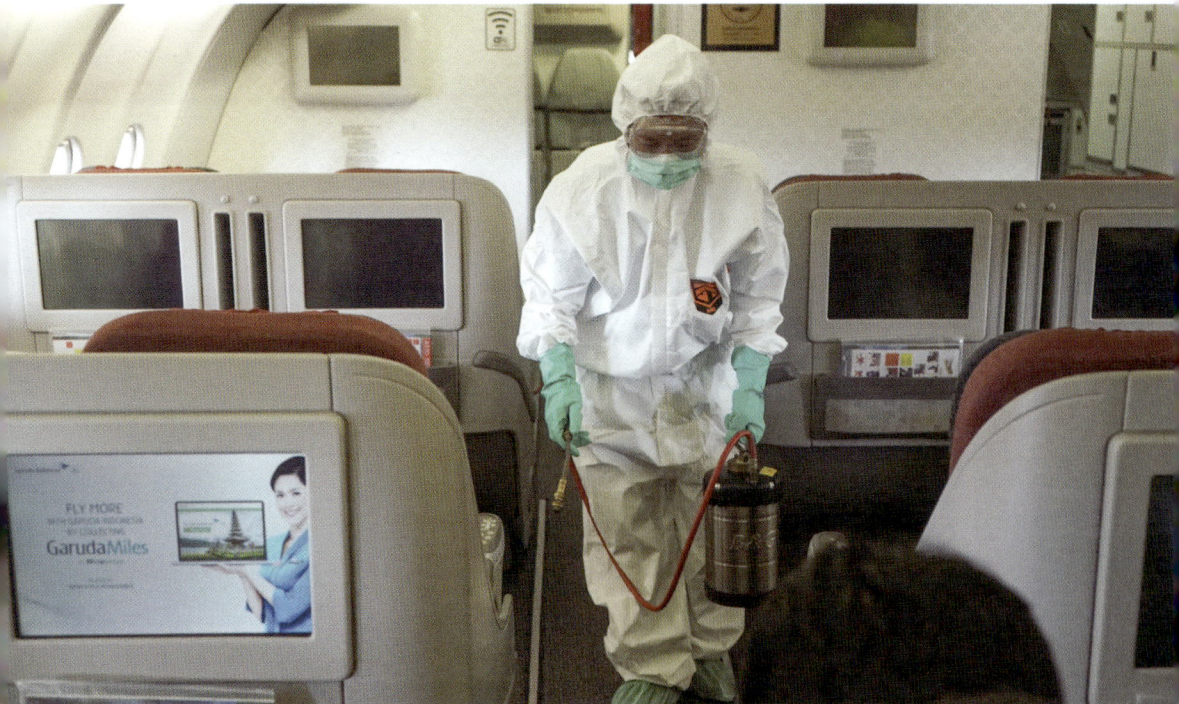

The outcome of the COVID-19 pandemic will greatly influence Garuda's future and we wish the airline all the best. (Garuda Indonesia)

Incidents and Accidents

On 17 November 1950, a Douglas C-47A with registration PK-DPB ran off the runway and hit a ditch during a landing at Surabaya Airport. There were three crew members and 23 passengers on board. Two crew members and two passengers were killed in the crash.

On 15 March 1952, a Convair CV-240 with registration PK-GCH and a Douglas DC-3 with registration PK-RCR were involved in a mid-air collision. Both aircraft landed safely, and there were no fatalities.

On 9 May 1952, a Douglas DC-3 with registration PK-DPA made a forced landing outside the airport of Palembang (South Sumatra) during take-off. There were no fatalities.

On 25 November 1954, a Douglas C-47A on a flight from Palembang (South Sumatra) to Jambi on the same island overran the runway on landing and came to a stop in muddy terrain. Pilot error (landing too far down the slippery runway and excessive speed) were considered to be the causes of the accident. There were no fatalities.

On 10 December 1958, a de Havilland Heron with registration PK-GHP was damaged beyond repair at the Jakarta Kemajoran Airport. There were no fatalities.

On 24 December 1959, a Douglas C-47A (DC-3) with registration PK-GDV, in flight from Palembang Talang Betoetoe Airport to Pangkal Pinang on Bangka Island was damaged beyond repair. A number 2 engine failed 13 minutes after take-off, forcing the crew to return to Palembang. The aircraft crashed into a swamp short of the Palembang runway. Failure of the right engine and a lack of precaution on the part of the pilot, together with bad weather conditions, were contributing factors. There were four people aboard the flight; one crew member was killed.

On 24 January 1961, a Douglas DC-3 with registration PK-GDI took off from Jakarta Kemajoran Airport for a flight to Bandung, Yogjakarta and Surabaya. The aircraft climbed to its cruising altitude of 3,500 feet to fly below the clouds. After 54 minutes, the crew asked permission to climb to flight level 95. The pilot was then instructed to contact Husein Tower, but the latter didn't acknowledge. The aircraft did not arrive at its destination and a day later, wreckage was found on the western slope of Mount Burangrang at an altitude of 5,400 feet. The attempt by the pilot to fly over mountainous terrain when unsure of his position and during bad weather conditions that restricted visibility were the causes of the accident. All 22 people on board were killed.

On 3 February 1961, a Douglas DC-3 with registration PK-GDY went missing while flying over the Java Sea on a flight from Surabaya Juanda Airport to Balikpapan Sepingan Airport. All five crew members and 21 passengers were believed to have perished.

On 29 December 1961, a Douglas DC-3 with registration PK-GDZ was damaged beyond repair. There were no fatalities.

On 27 February 1962, a Convair CV-240 with registration PK-GCB was damaged beyond repair at Palembang Airport. There were no fatalities.

On 5 April 1962, a Douglas C-47A (DC-3) with registration PK-GDM was damaged by fire at Jakarta Kemajoran Airport. There were no fatalities.

On 17 August 1962, a Convair CV-240 with registration PK-GCE was damaged beyond repair in Ambon.

On 14 May 1963, a Scottish Aviation Twin Pioneer with registration PK-GTC was damaged beyond repair.

On 20 September 1963, another Scottish Aviation Twin Pioneer with registration PK- GTB crashed into terrain on landing. Seven occupants were killed.

On 1 January 1966, two Douglas DC-3 aircraft (registrations PK-GDE and PK-GDU) collided while on approach into Palembang Airport and crashed into a swamp. All 34 occupants were killed.

On 16 February 1967, a Lockheed L-188C Electra with registration PK-GLB crashed on landing at Manada Airport (Sulawesi). The aircraft had left Jakarta on a flight to Manado via Surabaya and Makassar. On the second leg of the flight, bad weather at Makassar forced the pilot to return to Surabaya. The next day, the flight continued to Makassar and on to Manado. Weather information for Manado indicated a cloud base at 900 feet with 1.25 miles (2km) visibility. An approach to runway 18 was made, but after passing a hill 200 feet above runway elevation and 2,720 feet short of the threshold, the pilot realised he was too high and far left of the centreline. The nose was lowered, and the aircraft banked right to intercept the glidepath. The speed decreased below the 125 knots target threshold speed, and the aircraft, still banked to the right, landing heavily 156 feet short of the runway threshold. The undercarriage collapsed and the aircraft skidded and caught fire. Contributing factors to the accident were the 98ft-wide runway, which looks smaller from the pilot's point of view; the uneven pavement, which forces pilots to touch down as close as possible to the threshold; the marginal weather conditions prevailing at the moment of the landing, which forced the pilot to accomplish a tight circuit; and the relationship between the rate of sink and the negative thrust at low speed, which was not known to the pilots. Of the eight crew members and 84 passengers, 22 people died.

On 28 May 1968, a Convair 990 with registration PK-GJA, bound for Amsterdam with stops in Bombay, Karachi, Cairo and Rome, crashed in the village of Bilalpada (India) shortly after taking off from Bombay Santa Cruz Airport. All 29 people aboard died. In addition, there was one casualty on the ground. It was determined that the loss of control was the result of the partial or complete failure of all four engines during the initial climb. Investigators determined that during the stop in Bombay, the wrong type of fuel was transferred into the tanks of the aircraft. Instead of kerosene, the ground staff had fuelled the aircraft with regular petrol.

On 26 September 1972, a Fokker F27 Friendship with registration PK-GFP, crashed after having reached an altitude of 95 feet, taking off from runway 35 during a training flight at Jakarta Kemayoran Airport. The aircraft banked to the right of the centreline and crashed next to the runway. All three occupants were killed.

On 7 September 1974, a Fokker F27 Friendship crashed on approach at Tanjung Karang-Branti Airport (Lampung). The aircraft crashed short of the runway during an approach in limited visibility. The aircraft struck buildings near the runway and caught fire. Thirty-three out of 36 people on board perished.

On 24 September 1975, a Fokker F28 Fellowship 1000 with registration PK-GVC crashed on approach to Sultan Mahmud Badaruddin II Airport, struck a coconut tree on the downwind leg for a runway 28 approach. Visibility was very poor with fog over the runway. Twenty-five of the 61 occupants, including four crew members, perished in the crash.

On 11 July 1979, a Fokker F28 Fellowship 1000 with registration PK-GND on a flight from Palembang to Medan hit Mount Sibayak on approach to Medan Airport. All 61 people on board were killed.

On 28 March 1981, a McDonnell Douglas DC-9-32 with registration PK-GNJ was hijacked on a domestic flight from Palembang to Medan by five heavily armed hijackers. The hijackers diverted the flight to Penang and then to Bangkok. They demanded the release of 84 political prisoners in Indonesia. On the third day of the hijacking (31 March 1981), the aeroplane, parked at Don Mueang International Airport, was stormed by Indonesian commandos. One of the commandos was shot, probably by accident by one of his comrades. Also the pilot was shot. The rest of the hostages were released unharmed. Two of the hijackers surrendered to the Thai commandos, but they were killed by the Indonesian commandos on the aircraft taking them back to Jakarta.

On 20 March 1982, a Fokker F28 Fellowship 1000 with registration PK-GVK on a domestic flight from Jakarta Kemayoran Airport to Bandar Lampung overran the runway at Tanjung Karang-Branti Airport in bad weather. The aircraft subsequently burst into flames killing all 27 people on board.

On 30 December 1984, a Douglas DC-9-30 with registration PK-GNI on a domestic flight from Yogjakarta to Denpasar touched down 6,000 feet down the runway and overran through a ditch, trees and a fence at Ngurah Rai International Airport in Bali. The aircraft broke into three pieces and caught fire. All 75 occupants survived the crash.

On 4 April 1987, a Douglas DC-9-30 with registration PK-GNQ, on a domestic flight from Aceh to Medan, hit a pylon and crashed on approach to Polonia International Airport during bad weather. A possible windshear might have been the cause of the accident. There were 23 fatalities out of the 45 occupants.

On 13 June 1996, a McDonnell Douglas DC-10-30 with registration PK-GIE on an international flight from Fukuoka via Denpasar to Jakarta overran the runway at Fukuoka Airport in Japan, after aborting take-off well above rotation speed. The number 3 engine fuel line was severed, resulting in a fire and the destruction of the rear end of the aircraft. Three of the 275 people on board were killed. Pilot error and maintenance problems were determined to be the cause of the accident.

On 26 September 1997, an Airbus A300B4-200 with registration PK-GAI flying from Jakarta to Medan, crashed in Sibolangit, 18 miles short of Medan Airport in poor visibility, killing all 234 people on board.

On 16 January 2002, a Boeing 737-300 with registration PK-GWA en route from Lombok to Yogjakarta was forced to make an emergency landing but finally crashed in poor weather on the Solo River because of a double engine flameout caused by water and hail ingestion. After the flameout, the pilot decided to ditch the aircraft at a shallow point in the river to save the 60 occupants on board. A stewardess was killed. All passengers walked away from the crash site.

On 7 September 2004, human rights activist Munir Said Thalib was murdered on Garuda Indonesia flight 974, bound for Amsterdam. He was poisoned. Garuda's CEO at that time, Indra Setiawan, his deputy, Rohainil Aini, and pilot Pollycarpus Privanto were all convicted of this murder, although later investigation proved the involvement of the Indonesian secret service. Garuda was found negligent in failing to perform an emergency landing after it became clear Munir was ill and was ordered to pay compensation to Munir's widow.

On 7 March 2007, a Boeing 737-400 with registration PK-GZC flying from Jakarta to Yogjakarta overran the runway on landing at Adisucipto Airport in Yogjakarta and ended up in a rice paddy. Twenty-one of the 140 people on board were killed when the aircraft burst into flames.

On 16 August 2013, a Boeing 737-800 with registration PK-GMH experienced problems with the nose wheel. The aircraft landed safely. Nobody was injured.

On 3 February 2015, an ATR 72 with registration PK-GAG on a flight between Bali and Lombok overran the runway at Lombok International Airport on landing. There were no injuries, but the airport had to be closed for several hours. Investigation showed that the handling of the aircraft after touchdown was contrary to the wind condition, and the application of the right rudder and cross wind condition might have made the aircraft turn to the right.

On 1 February 2017, a Boeing 737-800 with registration PK-GNK on a domestic flight from Jakarta to Yogjakarta overran the runway at Adisucipto International Airport in Yogjakarta on landing in heavy rain. There were no injuries among the 199 passengers and five crew on board.

Garuda Fleet Details

Garuda historic fleet

	Total	First introduction	Retirement	Replaced by
Douglas DC-3	27	1949	1970	Fokker F27-200 and Lockheed Electra
Convair CV-240	8	1950	1965	Fokker F27-200
Consolidated PHY Catalina	Unknown	1950	1953	Not replaced by seaplane
Convair CV-340	8	1952	1968	Fokker F27-200
de Havilland Heron	14	1952	1956	
Convair CV-440	3	1956	1970	Fokker F27-200
Lockheed L-188 Electra	3	1960	1976	Boeing 737 Classic
Convair CV-990	3	1962	1975	Douglas DC-8-50
Scottish Aviation Twin Pioneer	Unknown	1962	1963	
Fokker F27-200	Unknown	1967	1975	Fokker F28 Mk 1000
Fokker F27-600	12	1969	1977	Fokker F28 Mk 1000
Fokker F28 Mk 1000	24	1969	1982	Fokker F28 Mk 3000
Douglas DC-8-30	4	1969	1975	
Douglas DC-9-30	25	1970	1993	Boeing 737 Classic
Douglas DC-8-50	6	1972	1980	Airbus A300
Fokker F28 Mk 3000	7	1973	1999	Boeing 737 Classic
Douglas DC-8-60	1	1974	1976	unknown
Douglas DC-10-30	26	1976	2005	Airbus A330
Fokker F28 Mk 4000	Unknown	1978	2001	Boeing 737 Classic
Boeing 747-200	33	1980	2003	Boeing 747-400
Airbus A300B4-200FF	8	1981	1999	Airbus A330
Boeing 737-300	29	1989	2014	Boeing 737-800
McDonnell Douglas DC-10-10	1	1989	1989	Not replaced, was on short-term lease
Lockheed L-1011 Tristar	1	1990	1990	Not replaced was on short-term lease
Airbus A300-600R	13	1990	1997	Airbus A330
McDonnell Douglas MD 11	18	1991	2001	Airbus A330

	Total	First introduction	Retirement	Replaced by
Boeing 747-100	7	1991	1993	Leased
Boeing 747-200M	1	1992	1995	Leased
Boeing 737-400	27	1993	2012	Boeing 737-800
Boeing 747-400	14	1994	2017	Boeing 777 -300ER
Boeing 747-300	11	1996	2009	Leased
Boeing 737-500	5	1997	2015	Boeing 737-800
Airbus A340-300	1	2000	2001	Airbus A330
Boeing 767-300ER	17	2002	2012	Leased
Boeing 767-200ER	2	2008	2009	Leased

Garuda fleet as of August 2020

	Current	On order
Airbus A330-200	7	
Airbus A330-300	17	
Airbus A330-900neo	3	11
ATR 72-600	13	
Boeing 737-800	73	
Boeing 737 Max 8	1	
Boeing 777-300ER	10	
Bombardier CRJ1000	18	
Airbus A330-200F		1
Boeing 737-500F	2	
Boeing 737-800BCF		2
TOTAL	144	14

Source: Garuda Indonesia presentation results for the first half of 2020.